LAUBACH WAY TO Reading 4

A time-tested method that has taught millions of adults to read

OTHER VOWEL SOUNDS AND CONSONANT SPELLINGS

IN HONOR OF
Elizabeth (Betty) Mooney Kirk
1914–2004
Co-author of *Laubach Way to Reading*

FRANK C. LAUBACH • ELIZABETH MOONEY KIRK • ROBERT S. LAUBACH

New Readers Press
ProLiteracy's publishing division

Laubach Way to Reading 4
ISBN 978-1-56420-920-7

New Readers Press
ProLiteracy's Publishing Division
104 Marcellus Street, Syracuse, New York 13204
www.newreaderspress.com

Printed in the United States of America
9 8 7 6 5 4

Proceeds from the sale of New Readers Press materials support professional development, training, and technical assistance programs of ProLiteracy that benefit local literacy programs in the U.S. and around the globe.

Developmental Editor: Terrie Lipke
Creative Director: Andrea Woodbury
Production Specialist: Maryellen Casey
Art and Design Supervisor: James P. Wallace
Illustrations: Tom McNeely and Drew Rose, represented by Wilkinson Studios, Inc.
Cover Design: Carolyn Wallace

Table of Contents

Laubach Way to Reading

Laubach Way to Reading is a basic reading and writing course for adults and young adults. Even students with little or no reading experience can begin learning with success from the very first lesson.

Laubach Way to Reading is a revision of the *New Streamlined English* series, which grew out of the late Dr. Frank C. Laubach's 40 years of pioneering work in literacy education. This revised series continues to use the distinctive method he developed to teach reading. Millions of people have successfully learned to read and write by using this series in volunteer tutor and adult education programs, public schools, prisons, and libraries.

Learning by association

The Laubach method starts with the known—the spoken word—and moves to the unknown—the written word—in easy steps that elicit the correct response from the student and reinforce it immediately. The emphasis is on learning by association rather than rote memory.

Sequential and structured

The series teaches basic reading and writing skills in a sequential and structured way. The learner progresses from the sounds and regular spellings of the consonants to those of the short vowels, the long vowels, and finally to irregular spellings and more difficult reading and writing skills.

Sound-symbol relationships are taught in charts with key words for a sound and spelling. The key words appear in meaningful context in a story following each chart. Each lesson continues with review of previous material, dictation, writing practice, and homework. The basic lesson structure remains very much the same throughout the series, giving both students and teachers a consistent pattern to follow.

Laubach Way to Reading has four skill books, eight correlated readers, and four workbooks. The skill books and the accompanying teacher's manuals are necessary to provide the comprehensive basic reading program, which includes vocabulary building, phonics, structural analysis, comprehension, and study skills. Writing exercises reinforce reading concepts and develop spelling skills.

Detailed teacher's manuals

Both English-speaking and English-as-a-second-language (ESL) students can use the skill books, but their teachers use different manuals. Teachers of English-speaking students use the *Laubach Way to Reading* manuals. ESL teachers use the *Laubach Way to English* manuals, which provide instruction in conversation skills as well as reading and writing. The detailed step-by-step instructions in the manuals make it possible for both teachers and volunteer tutors to use the series with ease and confidence.

ū

u–e = ū

	human	hū′ mun	human
	computer	com pūt′ er	computer
	huge	huje hūj	huge
	use	uze ūz	use
	amuse	u muze′ u mūz′	amuse

The Computer Age

afraid (u fraid')	fact
become (bē come')	game
machine (mu shene')	space (spase)
airplane (air' plane)	spaceship (spase' ship)
business (biz' ness)	everywhere (ev' ery where)
record (rec' ord)	

This is the age of the computer. A computer is a machine that works with facts like names and addresses. It works with facts like prices and lists of things in stores.

A computer can find answers to questions very quickly. This machine works much faster than a human. But a computer cannot think. A human must put facts into the machine. Then the human must tell the machine what to do with the facts.

Computers are used in business. Businesses use computers to keep records of sales. They use computers to write paychecks and to send bills. Banks use computers to keep records of money. Computers are used to help build huge buildings.

Computers run machines that make things. They run machines that make bread and cake. They help to make paper, cars, TVs, phones, and many other things.

Doctors use computers. Computers tell what sickness a person has. Then doctors know what cure is needed. Doctors do not have a cure for some sicknesses. Computers are helping doctors find cures.

Computers help you telephone other places quickly. A computer can tell what repairs your car needs. Computers help to teach many kinds of things. You can learn with computers in class or at home.

Computers help to amuse humans. Some of them amuse you by making music or pictures. Some computer games can amuse you at home. You can play these games on your own TV. Other computer games are so little that you can carry them with you.

This is both the computer age and the space age. Computers are used to build airplanes and spaceships. People are trained to fly airplanes and spaceships with the help of computers. On space flights, computers help keep spaceships on the right path in space.

Some computers do just one job. Some do many jobs. A computer that does many jobs may be huge or little. It may be so huge that it fills a big office. Or the computer may be as little as an egg.

The first computers cost a lot. But computers have become cheaper and cheaper. They have become so cheap that most businesses have them. Many people use computers at work and at home. Some homes even have more than one computer.

Computers help us in many ways. But they can be used to hurt us. Money can be stolen from banks and businesses by computers. Bombs can be made and dropped with the help of computers.

Some people say these machines are taking jobs away from humans. Computers *are* taking away some jobs and making others. But a person needs training for a computer job.

Some people are afraid of computers. They are afraid of machines with no feelings. They are afraid that humans will become cold and hard like these machines.

But we must not be afraid of computers. We live in a computer age. Computers are everywhere. We must learn to understand what they can do for us. And we must use them in the right ways.

Story Checkup

Answer each question with *yes* or *no*.

1. Does a computer work faster than a human? ________________
2. Does a computer have to be huge? ________________
3. Do some doctors use computers? ________________
4. Can computers be used to hurt us? ________________
5. Can a computer think? ________________
6. Are some people afraid of computers? ________________

form	print	social (sō' shul)	security (se cūr' i ty)

Some applications and business forms can be read by computers. On these forms, you fill in boxes. You print one letter or number in each box.

Fill in the form below. Print your own name, address, and other facts. You can find your Social Security number on your Social Security card. You need this number to get a job or to save money in a bank. You use it when you pay some taxes. If you do not have a Social Security number yet, do not fill in that part. In the last three parts, put an X in the right box.

PLEASE PRINT. USE CAPITAL LETTERS.

NAME

Last name First name

ADDRESS

Number Street

City State Zip code

Telephone number Social Security number

Age Sex Married? Born in U.S.A.?

M F Yes No Yes No

example (eg zam' pul), stress

Say the words. Circle the words with the sound ū as in *music*.

1. huge	hurry	use	us
2. Cuba	much	hurt	music
3. courage	business	computer	cure
4. church	human	Arthur	amuse
5. future	money	security	sentence

Say each word. Put the stress mark after the syllable that is stressed.

Examples:

human	hu' man	application	ap pli ca' tion
1. machine	ma chine	5. security	se cur i ty
2. afraid	a fraid	6. computer	com put er
3. amuse	a muse	7. radio	ra di o
4. music	mu sic	8. number	num ber

Read the word. Then write the two words that you see in it.

1. paycheck __________ __________
2. airplane __________ __________
3. spaceship __________ __________
4. everywhere __________ __________
5. understand __________ __________

Fill in each blank with the right word.

1. Computers are helping doctors find ____________________.
2. A ____________________ must put facts into the computer.
3. Some computer games can ____________________ you at home.
4. We live in an age of ____________________.
5. Businesses use computers to keep ____________________ of sales.

Read each word. Then write each word in the form that means more than one.

Example: tax taxes

1. business ____________________
2. sickness ____________________
3. address ____________________
4. box ____________________
5. airplane ____________________
6. price ____________________
7. class ____________________
8. fact ____________________
9. human ____________________

Write each of these words in the right blank.

address	business	game	human	machine	sickness

1. A computer is a ____________________.
2. A store is a ____________________.
3. A woman is a ____________________.
4. 325 York Street is an ____________________.
5. Hockey is a ____________________.
6. A cold is a ____________________.

ue = ū

ew = ū

	rescue	res′ cue	rescue
	barbecue	bar′ bu cue	barbecue
	continue	con tin′ ue	continue
	view	vew	view
	nephew	nef′ ew	nephew

A Family Reunion

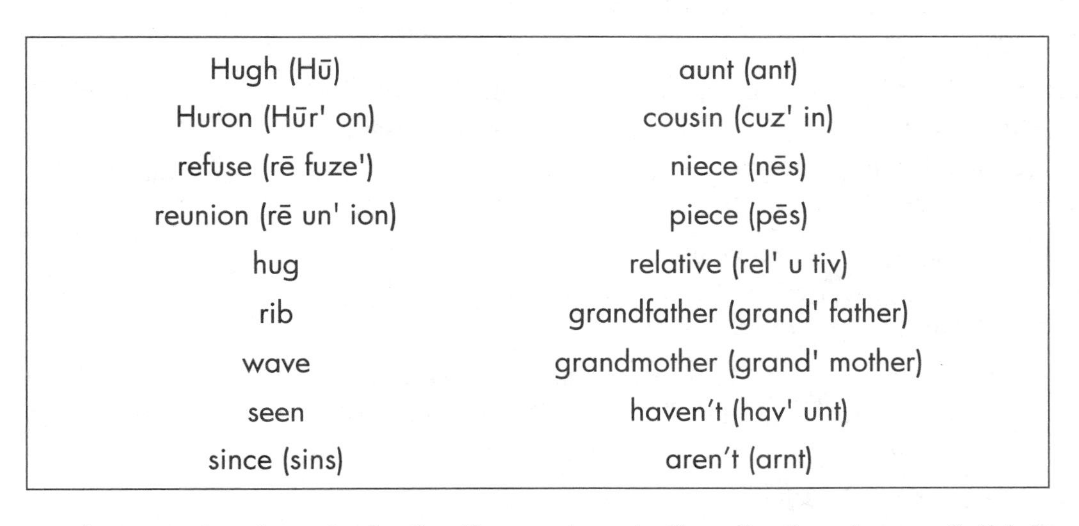

Hugh (Hū)	aunt (ant)
Huron (Hūr' on)	cousin (cuz' in)
refuse (rē fuze')	niece (nēs)
reunion (rē un' ion)	piece (pēs)
hug	relative (rel' u tiv)
rib	grandfather (grand' father)
wave	grandmother (grand' mother)
seen	haven't (hav' unt)
since (sins)	aren't (arnt)

Last weekend, we had a family reunion. At first, I refused to go. I didn't think anyone my age was going. But my mother felt hurt when I refused. So I went.

The reunion was at the home of my Aunt Mary and Uncle John. Aunt Mary is my mother's sister. At 17, I am her youngest nephew. This was a reunion of my mother's family.

Aunt Mary and Uncle John have a big home on Lake Huron. Their home has a lovely view of Lake Huron. We live just a few miles from them. But we don't have a view of Lake Huron.

My aunt and uncle were planning a big barbecue for Saturday. More than thirty relatives were coming. My parents and I went on Friday to help my aunt and uncle get ready.

On Saturday, relatives came from far and near. My grandmother and grandfather came from Florida. They have lived there since my grandfather retired. Grandmother gave me a big hug and kiss. She said, "Hugh, I haven't seen you since you were a boy. You have become a man!"

My brother and his wife came from Texas with their little girl. I was glad to see my three-year-old niece for the first time. She gave me a big hug and said, "I like my Uncle Hugh."

A few of my cousins came from Canada. My mother was glad to see her nephews and nieces. These cousins are not much older than I am. So I was glad that someone my age was there.

At the barbecue, we had a lot to eat. I had some potato salad, a piece of ham, and some barbecued ribs. I liked the ribs best.

But my Aunt Ellen will never eat barbecued ribs again. While she was eating, she began to argue. She was arguing with my father. Then she got a funny look on her face, and she stopped arguing.

"What's the matter?" I asked. But she was not able to answer. "A piece of meat must be stuck in her throat," I said to Dad.

I acted fast to rescue Aunt Ellen. I got behind her and gave her a big hug. Up came the piece of meat!

That was my first rescue of the day. Later, I rescued my little niece. She was playing with a few other children on the shore. When the waves came in, the children ran away from them. But a big wave hit my niece. The wave carried her into water over her head. I got to her first. She was not hurt. But I became the big man of the day.

That evening, my grandfather started telling family stories. Then other relatives told more stories. We continued telling stories far into the night. I learned some things that I didn't know before.

The reunion continued the next day. I went fishing with a few of my cousins. When everyone was ready to leave, there were more kisses and hugs.

On the way home, my mother said to me, "I had a lot of fun this weekend. I haven't seen so many of my relatives since your brother's wedding. You're glad that you went to the reunion, aren't you, Hugh?"

"Yes, I am," I said. "I'm glad that I didn't refuse to go. In fact, I hope that we will continue to have family reunions."

Hugh's relatives in this story are his:

grandfather	Aunt Mary	Aunt Ellen	father	brother	niece
grandmother	Uncle John		mother	brother's wife	cousins

Write the answer. Which of Hugh's relatives—

1. had the reunion at their home on Lake Huron? ______________________________
2. came from Florida? ______________________________
3. came from Texas? ______________________________
4. came from Canada? ______________________________
5. said, "Hugh, I haven't seen you since you were a boy"? ______________________________
6. choked on a piece of meat? ______________________________
7. did Hugh see for the first time? ______________________________
8. started telling family stories? ______________________________
9. did Hugh rescue from the lake? ______________________________
10. said, "You're glad that you went to the reunion, aren't you?" ______________________________

In what order did these things happen?
Put a number by each sentence to show the right order.

_____ Relatives came from near and far.

_____ Hugh acted fast to rescue his aunt.

_____ Hugh and his parents went to Aunt Mary's home.

_____ Aunt Ellen began to argue with Hugh's father.

_____ Grandfather started telling family stories.

_____ A big wave hit Hugh's niece.

_____ Aunt Ellen choked on a piece of meat.

_____ Hugh and some of his cousins went fishing.

_____ Hugh rescued his niece from the lake.

choke	press	minute (min' ut)
fist	breathe	object (ob' ject)

When a Person Chokes

Each year, many people die from choking. A person chokes when he is eating and something gets stuck in his throat. If you see this happen, you can save a life. But you have to act fast. A person will die in four to six minutes if he can't breathe.

Signs of choking

- The person cannot breathe or speak.
- He may put his hands to his throat or look afraid.
- His face may turn a funny color.

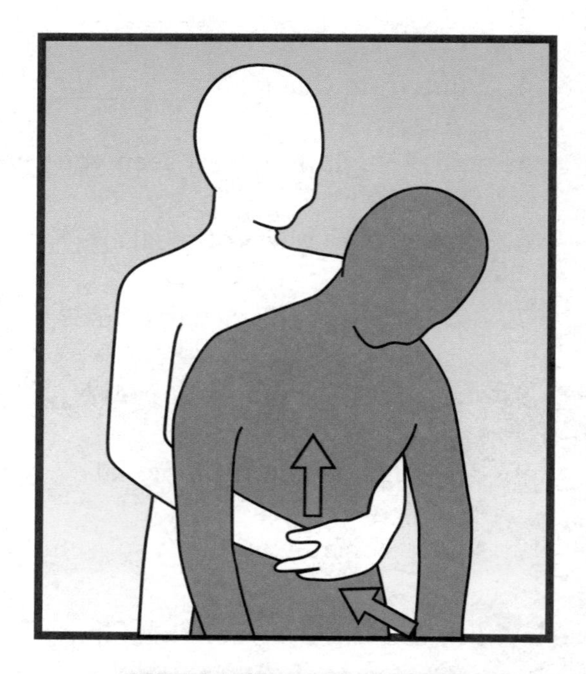

If the person can breathe or speak a little, let him try to get the object up by himself. If he cannot get the object up after a few minutes, you can help.

If the person cannot breathe or speak, you must act quickly to help him.

What to do

1. Stand behind the choking person.
2. Make a fist with one of your hands.
3. Put your fist just below the person's ribs, as the picture shows.
4. With your other hand, press your fist in and up quickly. Press hard enough so that air comes up. This will bring the object up from the person's throat.
5. The object may come up after you press the first time. But you may have to press again and again.

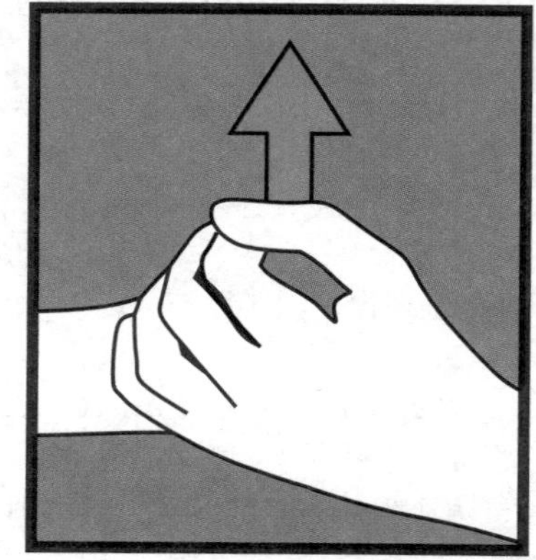

Practice

Say the words. Circle the words with the sound ū as in *few* and *argue*.

1. Hugh	hug	huge	nephew
2. aunt	view	cousin	continue
3. refuse	argue	minute	barbecue

Say each word. Put the stress mark after the syllable that is stressed.

1. rescue	res cue	4. nephew	neph ew
2. barbecue	bar be cue	5. continue	con tin ue
3. relative	rel a tive	6. refuse	re fuse

Homework

Read the word. Write the two words that it comes from.

1. didn't	________	________	5. I'm	________	________
2. haven't	________	________	6. you're	________	________
3. what's	________	________	7. don't	________	________
4. aren't	________	________	8. can't	________	________

These words are the names of some relatives. Write one word in each blank.

aunt   uncle   niece   nephew   cousin   grandmother   grandfather

1. Your mother's sister or your father's sister ____________________
2. Your aunt's child or your uncle's child ____________________
3. Your brother's son or your sister's son ____________________
4. Your mother's brother or your father's brother ____________________
5. Your mother's mother or your father's mother ____________________

oo

food

oo

	room	room	room
	pool	pool	pool
	school	skool	school
	noon	noon	noon
	soon	soon	soon
	too	too	too

A First Apartment

move (moov)	mind (mīnd)
Hoover (Hoov' er)	quiet (quī' et)
O'Toole (Ō Tool')	those (thoze)
afternoon (after noon')	isn't (iz' unt)
bedroom (bed' room)	together (too geth' er)
roommate (room' mate)	forever (for ev' er)
safe	landlord (land' lord)
swim	Sunday (Sun' day)

Kitty O'Toole had her first job. She had just finished business school. The school had helped her get the job.

Kitty was living with her parents. She wanted an apartment of her own. She told her parents, "I have finished school, and I have a job. I want to be on my own. I have made up my mind. I am going to move into an apartment soon."

Her father said, "You can't afford an apartment. You don't make enough money to pay for food and rent. Here at home you don't pay any rent for your room. You just pay for food."

"We think you're too young to live by yourself," said Kitty's mother. "It isn't safe these days. We want you to live at home. You are safer here."

But Kitty O'Toole had made up her mind. "I'm 19 years old," she told them. "It's time for me to be on my own. You can't keep me here at home forever. On Sunday, I'm going to look for an apartment."

Kitty looked at the ads for apartments in the Sunday paper. Kitty liked to swim. She hoped to find an apartment in a building with a swimming pool. But she soon gave up that idea. The rent for those apartments was too much for her. There were only a few places that she was able to afford. And those were not in a very safe part of the city.

Kitty went to look at those places anyway. She left home before noon. She spent Sunday afternoon looking at apartments. But she didn't find one she liked.

"What shall I do?" Kitty asked herself. "I don't like the apartments I can afford, and I can't afford the ones I like. I need a roommate to share the rent."

Kitty started looking for a roommate. In the next few weeks, she spoke to people at work and at church. She spoke to friends from school. "Do you know anyone who needs a roommate?" she asked. But no one did.

At last, a friend told Kitty that Jane Hoover was looking for a roommate. Kitty had met Jane at a school party. But she didn't know her very well. Kitty O'Toole phoned Jane Hoover at work the next morning. They agreed to have lunch together that noon.

Kitty and Jane liked each other right away. They learned that they liked many of the same things. They liked the same kind of music. And they both liked to swim.

Jane said that she liked peace and quiet. "Me too!" Kitty said. "Sometimes I stay up late at night, but I play my radio quietly. And I don't give wild parties."

Kitty added, "I like to spend some time by myself. I want a roommate who will understand that." Jane said she felt the same way.

Kitty and Jane agreed to look for an apartment together. They spent three weekends looking. They looked at 22 apartments. Some cost too much. Some didn't look very safe or clean.

Late one Sunday afternoon, Jane said, "I'm tired. Let's quit for today."

"Oh, come on!" Kitty said. "Let's try one more."

The next apartment they looked at was just right. It had two bedrooms. From the living room, there was a view of a park. The kitchen needed paint. But the building was clean and quiet. And the rent was not too high.

Kitty and Jane asked the landlord a lot of questions. "Is there a bus stop near here? Are there any stores? Is the building safe at night?" The landlord answered yes to those questions. Then Kitty asked, "There isn't a swimming pool in the building, is there?"

"No," the landlord said. "But there is a pool in the park."

The two young women made up their minds in a hurry. "We'll take it!" they said. They paid the rent and got the key.

Kitty and Jane moved into the apartment together. They shared the cost of the rent, telephone, lights, and food. Each of them got a bed from home for her bedroom. Kitty's parents let her take some dishes and pans. The Hoovers let Jane take a rug and an old toaster. Jane had her own TV, and Kitty had a computer. They shopped for a used sofa, a table, and some chairs. They made end tables from boxes. Jane made curtains, and Kitty painted the kitchen.

After they had worked hard for two months, the apartment looked nice. Kitty and Jane were pleased. "My parents said I was too young to be on my own," said Kitty.

"My parents said the same thing," said Jane. "Parents want to keep you at home forever, don't they?"

"Yes, they do," said Kitty. "Let's ask them to dinner soon. We'll show them that we were right."

Write one or two sentences to answer each question.

1. Why did Kitty want an apartment of her own? ______________________

____

____

2. Why did her parents want her to live at home? ______________________

____

____

3. Why did Kitty look for a roommate? ______________________

____

____

4. What kinds of things did Kitty and Jane both like? ______________________

____

____

5. What kind of apartment did they rent? ______________________

____

____

6. What costs did Kitty and Jane share? ______________________

____

____

7. In what ways did they get the things they needed for their apartment?

____

____

____

heat	utilities (ū til' i tēz)
furnished (fur' nisht)	deposit (dē poz' it)
unfurnished (un fur' nisht)	

Ads can help you find apartments for rent. The furnished ones have beds, tables, chairs, and other things. The unfurnished ones do not.

Utilities are lights, heat, and water.

A security deposit is money you pay when you move in. You get it back when you move away if you have not broken anything.

Read these ads, and write short answers to the questions.

APARTMENTS—FURNISHED

2080 Baker Street. 2-bedroom apartment on second floor of quiet family home. Security deposit. Utilities paid. $600. 424-1960.

Court Street Arms. 3 rooms. Clean. No pets. Heat paid. $120 a week. 434-1083.

APARTMENTS—UNFURNISHED

1216 Circle Drive. 4 rooms, just painted. 5 minutes from university. Landlord pays everything. $575. Hurry. 427-8060.

223 First Street. 3 bedrooms. On bus line. 424-1492.

Hill Top Apartments. Country living 20 minutes from city. Swimming pool & game room. 1- and 2-bedroom apartments, $675 and up. Business office open 9-5. 699-4051.

North Side. Woman needs roommate to share rent & utilities. Own bedroom. No smokers. $350. 426-3530 after 6 p.m.

765 Oak Street. 2 bedrooms, eat-in kitchen. Near bus stop, stores. $525, pay own utilities. Security deposit. 424-6734.

26 Union Place. 2 bedrooms, large living room. Children OK. Parking. $595. Heat, hot water. 424-1489.

1. Is the apartment on Circle Drive furnished or unfurnished? ____________________

2. Where is the furnished apartment in a family home? ____________________

3. Who pays the utilities at 765 Oak Street, the landlord or the renter? ____________________

   Does the renter have to pay a security deposit at this place? ____________________

4. Where is the rent paid weekly? ____________________

5. Which apartments have a pool? ____________________

6. What fact comes last in each of these ads? ____________________

7. What time can you phone the woman who wants a roommate? ____________________

8. What utilities does the landlord pay for at 26 Union Place? ____________________

9. Where does an apartment cost the most? ____________________

begin (bē gin')

Say the words. Circle the words with the sound *oo* as in *food*.

1. soon	spoke	noon	north
2. food	future	for	school
3. phone	pool	too	tore
4. more	move	room	music
5. Hoover	Hugo	O'Toole	United

Put *un-* at the beginning of each word to make another word. Write the word.

Example: furnished unfurnished

1. finished ____________________
2. married ____________________
3. painted ____________________
4. answered ____________________
5. loved ____________________
6. used ____________________
7. locked ____________________
8. paid ____________________

Fill in each blank with one of the words that begins with *un-*.
(You may use the example word in your answers.)

1. The child felt ____________________.
2. The rent is cheaper for an ____________________ apartment.
3. The work I started last week is still ____________________.
4. The back door was ____________________ when I came home.
5. Two ____________________ girls shared the apartment.
6. John has a lot of ____________________ bills.
7. Jane got some ____________________ chairs and painted them herself.
8. The question is ____________________.
9. If I take the ____________________ can of paint back to the store, can I get my money back?

root

Drop the ending from each word. Write the root word.

1. swimming ____________
2. renter ____________
3. quietly ____________
4. dishes ____________
5. agreed ____________
6. shared ____________
7. weekly ____________
8. choking ____________
9. toaster ____________
10. cities ____________
11. shopped ____________
12. smoker ____________
13. youngest ____________
14. parties ____________

Read the word. Then write the two words you see in it.

1. everywhere ____________ ____________
2. spaceship ____________ ____________
3. bedroom ____________ ____________
4. afternoon ____________ ____________
5. landlord ____________ ____________
6. roommate ____________ ____________
7. grandmother ____________ ____________
8. airplane ____________ ____________
9. Sunday ____________ ____________
10. forever ____________ ____________

Write two questions that Kitty and Jane asked the landlord.

1. ____
2. ____

u–e = oo
ue = oo

June

u–e = oo

blue

ue = oo

	flute	flute floot	flute
	salute	su lute su loot′	salute
	rule	rule rool	rule
	rude	rude rood	rude
	true	true	true

The Flag

flag	parade (pu rade')	leaf
drum	remove (rē move')	goes (gōz)
star	honor (on' er)	heart (hart)
stripe	bugle (bū' gul)	holiday (hol' i day)
July (Joo lȳ')	maple (mā' pul)	daytime (day' time)

People show their love for their country when they honor their flag. The bright colors of the flag stand for the country, its people, and its ideas.

The flag of the United States is red, white, and blue. Red stands for courage. White stands for honor. And blue stands for justice. The flag has 13 stripes of red and white. These stripes stand for the first 13 states. The top left corner of the flag is blue with 50 white stars. The stars stand for the 50 states in the United States today. We sometimes give the U.S. flag a name. One name we use is the Stars and Stripes.

Some people say that a leader of the country made the first U.S. flag. That may be true. Other people say that a woman made the first flag in her home. That may be true. We may never know the true story.

In the United States, people honor their flag on June 14. June 14 is Flag Day. On June 14, people fly the flag on their homes, businesses, and city buildings.

The flag of Canada is white with a red maple leaf on it. On each side of the maple leaf is a red stripe. The red maple leaf stands for the country of Canada.

In both Canada and the United States, people fly the flag on holidays. In the United States, one big holiday is the Fourth of July. The Fourth of July honors the day the country was born. That day was July 4, 1776.

A big holiday in Canada is Canada Day on July 1. This holiday honors the day that the country was united. That day was July 1, 1867.

There are many parades on Canada Day and the Fourth of July. Many bands march in the parades. The bands have drums, bugles, and flutes. The bands march to the drums. The bugles and flutes play march music. You can hear the drums, bugles, and flutes from far away.

A person carrying the flag marches at the head of the parade. When your country's flag goes by, you stand up and salute. A man removes his hat. He salutes by placing his hand over his heart. A woman does not remove her hat. She salutes by placing her hand over her heart, too.

It is rude not to stand when the flag of any country goes by. It is rude not to salute the flag of your own country. It is rude for a man not to remove his hat for his country's flag.

Most countries have rules for honoring the flag. Here are a few rules that many countries follow:

1. You may fly the flag in the daytime. If there is a light on the flag, you may fly it at night, too.
2. Do not fly the flag in the rain.
3. Do not let the flag touch the floor.
4. Do not throw away an old flag. Burn it with care.

These rules will help you honor the flag and show love for your country.

Story Checkup

Fill in each blank with the right word or number from the story.

1. In the U.S. flag, there are ____________________ stars.

   Each star stands for a ____________________.

   The ____________________ stand for the first 13 states.

   Flag Day in the United States is on ____________________.

2. The flag of Canada is ____________________ with a ____________________ maple leaf.

   On each side of the maple leaf is a red ____________________.

   Canada Day is on ____________________.

club	per	concert (con' sert)	language (lang' gwij)
main	picnic (pic' nic)	fireworks (fire' works)	Thursday (Thurz' day)
meet	zoo		

Your paper can help you find things to do in your free time. Read this part of the Center City paper. Then fill in the blanks.

Center City Weekly Bugle

THINGS TO DO THIS WEEK

SUNDAY, JULY 4

Children's Petting Zoo opens today. Zoo will be open every Sunday 1-5 p.m. Maple Road near Oak Hill. $1 per person.

Dinner at First Union Church, 121 Main Street. After-dinner speaker: Dr. Hugo Black, "Honoring God and Country." 6:30 p.m. $5.50.

MONDAY, JULY 5

Fourth of July parade, six marching bands, starts at 10 a.m. Marchers meet at high school at 9 a.m. Watch the parade as it goes up Main Street to Jones Park. Bring your flags!

Picnic at Jones Park following the parade. Bicycle races, games and prizes, singing. Bring your own food. Hot & cold drinks on sale at picnic.

Fireworks and band concert at Lake Shore Park, 9 p.m. $2 per car.

THURSDAY, JULY 8

Free swimming lessons at Jones Park pool on Thursday afternoons and evenings. Phone park office to sign up. 806-3811.

Evening classes at King's College: English as a second language, 7-9 in Building 3. Sign language, 7-10 at the Learning Center for the Deaf.

Club meeting. Blue Lake Fishing & Hunting Club meets at 8 p.m. in the Hoover Building, Room 16.

FRIDAY, JULY 9

Bake sale put on by Parents of the Handicapped. North Way Shopping Center, noon to 6 p.m.

Barbecue at Valley Fire Department to raise money for rescue truck. 5:30-8:30 p.m. $10 per person.

SATURDAY, JULY 10

Morning-to-night band concert, 15 bands & 32 singers. Rock, blues, & country music. Lake Shore Park, 10 a.m. to 10 p.m. $12 per person.

Camp for boys and girls ages 6-18 July 10-July 24, at Maple Leaf State Park. Run by Camp Fire of Center City, 813-6080.

Garden Club weekly meeting at Porter Rose Garden, 2 p.m.

1. The Children's Petting Zoo opens on July ____________.
2. The Fourth of July ____________ goes up Main Street.
3. At the picnic, you can buy drinks, but you must bring your own ____________.
4. If six people go to the fireworks in the same car, they must pay ____________.
5. You can get free swimming lessons on ____________ afternoons and evenings.
6. The sign language class meets at the Learning Center for the ____________.
7. The hunting and fishing club meets at ____________ on Thursday.
8. The fire department is having a barbecue to raise money for a ____________ truck.
9. The concert on July 10 lasts from ____________ to ____________.

Say the words. Circle the words with the sound *oo* as in *blue* and *food*.

1.	rule	drum	room	hurt
2.	tree	too	true	club
3.	June	Jane	noon	bugle
4.	pool	school	July	few
5.	flute	salute	amuse	Thursday

Say each word. Put the stress mark after the syllable that is stressed.

1.	parade	pa rade
2.	remove	re move
3.	bugle	bu gle
4.	holiday	hol i day
5.	July	Ju ly
6.	Thursday	Thurs day
7.	picnic	pic nic
8.	maple	ma ple
9.	concert	con cert

Write each of these words after its meaning.

barbecue concert holiday parade reunion

1. Bands and people marching in a line: ____________________
2. A picnic at which meat is roasted over an open fire: ____________________
3. A day when businesses are closed and most people do not work: ____________________
4. A show in which people sing or play music: ____________________
5. A time when people come together again: ____________________

Write *yes* if the sentence is true. Write *no* if the sentence is not true.

__________ 1. On the U.S. flag, white stands for honor.

__________ 2. The stars on the U.S. flag are blue.

__________ 3. Helen Keller made the first U.S. flag.

__________ 4. Stars and Stripes is a name used for the flag of Canada.

__________ 5. The red maple leaf stands for the country of Canada.

__________ 6. By honoring the flag, you show love for your country.

Read each word. Then write each word in the form that means more than one.

1. country ____________________
2. holiday ____________________
3. parade ____________________
4. city ____________________
5. story ____________________
6. bugle ____________________
7. family ____________________
8. flute ____________________

Write two rules for honoring your country's flag.

1. ____

____

2. ____

____

ew = oo

chew

ew = oo

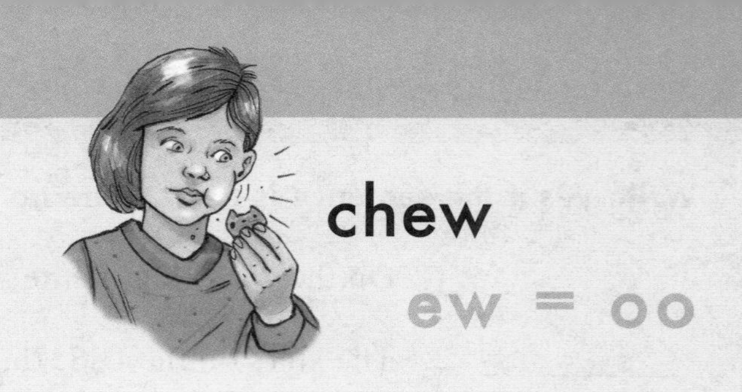

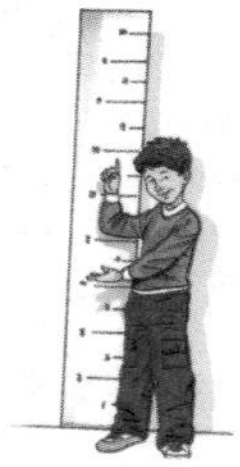	grew	grew	grew
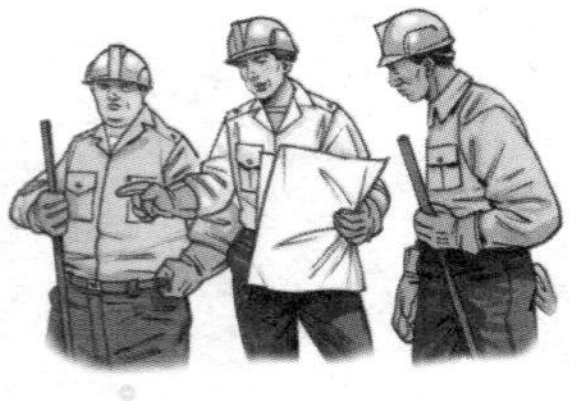	crew	crew	crew
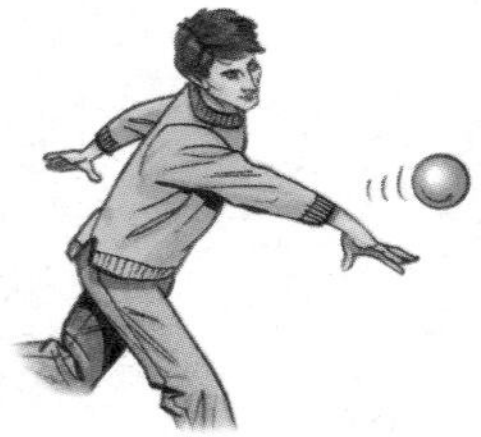	threw	threw	threw
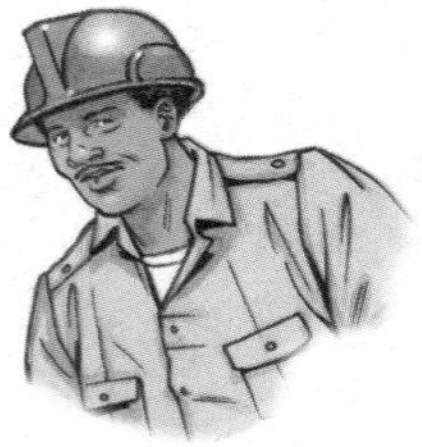	Lewis	Lew′ is	Lewis
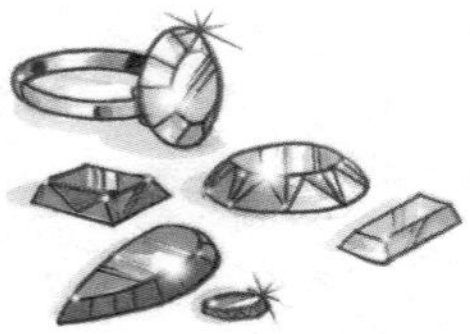	jewels	jew′ ulz	jewels
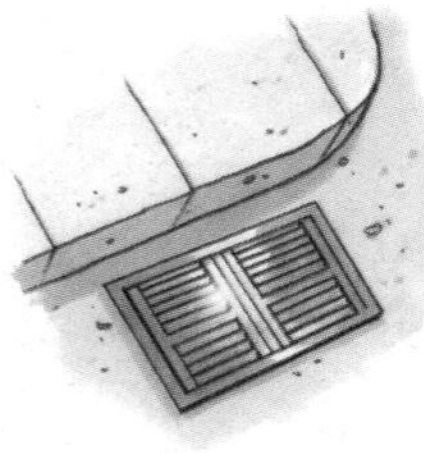	sewer	sew′ er	sewer

The Family Jewels

rich	dirt	until (un til')
poor	step	leftover (left' over)
cool	grow (grōw)	Judy (Joo' dy)
Luke	leaves (leavz)	

Lewis Burns came from a poor family. He grew up with very little money. As a child, Lewis said to himself, "When I grow up, I will not be poor. When I grow up, I will have a fine car. My wife will wear jewels. We will have a fine home."

Lewis had this dream as he grew up. He went to school until his father died. Then Lewis had to grow up in a hurry. He quit school and went to work.

Lewis worked for the city on the sewers. He was on a work crew. The crew of workers cleaned the sewers. Dirt and leaves got into the sewers. The work crew used a machine to remove the dirt and leaves. The machine threw the dirt and leaves into a truck.

It was a dirty job. But Lewis went to work every day in clean clothes. The crew laughed at him. "Look at Lewis," they said. "He looks like a cool cat in the morning. But by evening he looks like a sewer rat!"

"That's OK," said Lewis. "I won't be a sewer rat forever."

When Lewis was 20, he met Judy. Judy's family wasn't rich. But they had more money than Lewis's family. Judy grew up with nice clothes and other things she wanted.

"I love Judy," Lewis said to himself. "But she won't want to marry a sewer rat. I must stop seeing Judy."

Judy had another view. She told her parents, "Lewis may be poor, but he is a fine man. He loves me, and I love him. If we both work hard, we will have enough money to marry."

Judy and Lewis got married. Judy worked until Lewis Jr. was born. Then two years later, baby Luke was born.

A few years passed. Lewis still worked on the city crew. The children grew bigger. Judy stayed at home with them.

Judy looked for ways to save money. She never threw anything away. She never threw food away. She used leftovers for another meal. She never threw old clothes away. She used them to make clothes for Lewis Jr. and Luke.

The Burns family was getting by. They had enough money to live on, but they didn't own their home. They didn't have a car. They had enough food to eat, but Judy didn't wear fine jewels. Sometimes Lewis remembered his old dream.

One hot day, as Lewis came up the steps, he heard Luke crying. Judy was giving dinner to the children. "Chew your meat well," she said to Luke. "Chew your meat, or you will choke on it."

"I don't like this meat," said the boy.

"I worked hard to buy that meat, so eat it!" Lewis yelled. "And do what your mother says! Chew it well!" After he yelled at his son, Lewis felt bad. But he didn't say anything until dinner was over.

After dinner, the family sat on the steps. It was cooler there. They sat on the steps and had a cool drink. They watched the traffic go by.

"You don't have much of a life in this hot city," Lewis said to Judy. "I wanted to give you a fine home and jewels. But I haven't. We are nearly as poor as my parents were. And we will never be rich."

Judy hugged her husband and kissed him. Then she hugged her two boys. "These are my jewels, Lewis," she said. "You and the boys are my jewels. I am a happy wife and mother. We are rich, not poor."

Story Checkup

Answer each question with one or two sentences.

1. What was Lewis's dream? ______________________________

____

2. In what ways did Judy save money? ______________________________

____

3. Do you agree with Judy that she and Lewis are rich? ______________________________

____

trash
pickup (pick' up)
public (pub' lic)
report (rē port')
emergency (ē mer' jen sy)
information (in for mā' shun)

Lewis Burns worked for the public works department in his city. A city has many offices and departments. They give services to people who live in the city.

Sometimes you need to phone one of these offices for help or information. You can look up the number in the telephone directory. Look under the name of your city.

Here is the listing for some of the city offices where Lewis lived. Read the questions below, and look up the telephone numbers in the listing.

OAK PARK—CITY OF

EMERGENCY NUMBERS
Fire 911 Police 911

COURTS—Public Office Building
Information **342-4641**
Traffic Court **342-4655**
FIRE DEPARTMENT
To Report a Fire **911**
HUMAN RIGHTS OFFICE
Public Office Building **342-6072**
JAIL—595 Oak Street **325-6112**
MUSIC CENTER
220 Main Street
Box Office **363-7800**
PARKS DEPARTMENT
319 Hoover Street
Information **342-4051**
Sullivan Zoo
2763 Maple Drive **342-7447**
POLICE DEPARTMENT
595 Oak Street
Emergency **911**
Other Police Business
Bicycle Licenses **325-6151**
Missing Persons **325-7087**
PUBLIC WORKS DEPARTMENT
2861 Mason Street
Ice & Snow **342-6650**
Sewers & Street Cleaning **342-6651**
Street Repair **342-6652**
Trash Pickup **342-6653**
SCHOOLS
Oak Park Public Schools, Main Office
426 Freedom Circle **342-6014**

What number do you phone—

________ 1. to report a fire?

________ 2. to get the police in an emergency?

________ 3. to ask when the public swimming pools are open?

________ 4. to ask when the trash is picked up?

________ 5. to report a missing person?

________ 6. to ask what time a concert starts?

________ 7. to get information on night classes?

________ 8. to get someone to clean your sewers?

________ 9. to get information on the city courts?

________ 10. to report that your trash was not picked up?

opposite (op' u zit)

Say the words. Circle the words with the sound *oo* as in *chew, food,* and *June.*

1. grew	grow	crew	cure
2. Lewis	lunch	June	lake
3. throw	true	third	threw
4. Judy	rude	music	study
5. jewel	union	Luke	until

In each line, circle the word that means the opposite of the first word.

Example:

fast	quick	(slow)	first
1. poor	sad	happy	rich
2. dirty	funny	clean	pretty
3. hot	cold	high	sick
4. big	huge	little	short
5. young	nice	rude	old
6. continue	say	stop	question

Drop the ending from each word. Write the root word.

1. dirty ____________________
2. meeting ____________________
3. speaker ____________________
4. cooler ____________________
5. bigger ____________________
6. nearly ____________________
7. remembered ____________________
8. died ____________________
9. married ____________________
10. hugged ____________________
11. kissed ____________________
12. getting ____________________
13. giving ____________________
14. missing ____________________

above (u buv')

Say each word. Put the stress mark after the syllable that is stressed.

1. public pub lic
2. report re port
3. emergency e mer gen cy
4. dirty dirt y
5. sewers sew ers
6. information in for ma tion
7. until un til
8. jewels jew els

Fill in each blank with one of the words in the list above.

1. Lewis stayed in school ____________________ his father died.
2. Then Lewis got a job with the ____________________ works department.
3. Dirt and leaves got in the ____________________.
4. Cleaning the sewers was a ____________________ job.
5. To Judy, her husband and children are her ____________________.
6. What number do you phone to get the police in an ____________________?
7. Do you phone the same number to ____________________ a fire?
8. Where can you get ____________________ on night classes in the city?

Answer each question below with the name of a city department.
Where do you phone—

1. to report that a building is burning? ____
2. to report that something was stolen from you? ______________________________________

ū or oo

In some words, both ways are right.

	news	nūz or nooz	news
	Duke	Dūk or Dook	Duke
	student	stū′ dent or stoo′ dent	student
	tutor	tū′ ter or too′ ter	tutor
S M T W T F S 1 2 3 4 5 6 7 8 9 10 11 12 13 14 15 16 17 18 19 20 21 22 23 24 25 26 27 28 29 30 31	Tuesday	Tūz′ day or Tooz′ day	Tuesday
	avenue	av′ e nū or av′ e noo	avenue

A New Start

math	stupid (stū' pid)	believe (bē leve')
coach	newspaper (news' paper)	interest (in' ter est)
knew (new)	Newman (New' mun)	

Duke Miller was a student at Lake Avenue High School. When he got his report card on Tuesday, he felt very blue. "Another *F* in math!" he said to himself. "It's no use! I will never pass this stupid class! I'm going to quit school and get a job!"

Duke needed math to finish high school. He did well enough in his other classes. But math didn't interest him. He didn't understand it. And that made him feel stupid.

After school that day, Duke went to the office of the *Oak Park News*. He hoped to find a job in the press room. That was where the newspaper was printed. Duke asked to speak to Jack Newman, who ran the press room. Duke knew Mr. Newman from church camp. Mr. Newman was the sports coach there.

Duke told Mr. Newman that he was looking for a job. "But you're still a student, aren't you?" asked Mr. Newman.

"Yes, I'm a student. But I'm thinking of quitting school," Duke answered. "I'll be 16 next Tuesday. I'll be old enough to quit then."

"What's the matter with school?" asked Mr. Newman.

"It's the stupid math class!" Duke said. "I can't pass it no matter what I do. But I don't need math to run a printing press, do I?"

"Yes, Duke, I'm afraid you do," said Mr. Newman. "Anyway, 16 is too young to work on newspaper presses. You had better finish school first."

"I can't stand it any more," Duke said. "Math makes me feel stupid."

As the sports coach at church camp, Mr. Newman had spent a lot of time with Duke. He knew that Duke was not stupid. He believed that Duke just needed some help. "What you need is a tutor in math," he told Duke.

"My family can't afford a tutor," said Duke.

Mr. Newman said, "I'll be your tutor. You can pay me by babysitting my five-year-old son on Saturday mornings. My wife and I both work then."

Duke began going to Mr. Newman's home on Tuesday and Thursday evenings for his math lessons. The Newmans lived on Second Avenue, not far from Duke's home on Fourth Avenue.

Mr. Newman never made Duke feel stupid. He knew that Duke was interested in sports. So he asked Duke many questions on sports. Duke had to use math to find the answers. At last, Duke began to think that math was interesting. And he began to understand it.

Duke started doing his math lessons at school, too. By the end of the year, he was passing math. He went to his tutor with his report card. "I have some great news for you, Coach!" said Duke. "I passed! I got a *C* in math! See what you did for me!"

"You did most of it yourself," Mr. Newman said. "I just believed in you."

Duke smiled. "And thanks to you, I believe in myself, too."

Story Checkup

Write the story in a few sentences. Tell the main ideas.

calendar (cal' en der)	Wednesday (Wenz' day)
January (Jan' ū ār y)	birthday (birth' day)

JANUARY 2014						
Sunday	Monday	Tuesday	Wednesday	Thursday	Friday	Saturday
			1 New Year's Day	2	3	4
5	6	7	8	9	10	11
12	13	14	15	16	17	18
19	20 Martin Luther King Jr. Day	21	22	23	24	25
26	27	28	29	30	31	

Look at this calendar for January 2014, and answer these questions.

1. What holiday is on the first Wednesday of January 2014? ________________

2. Is New Year's Day on Wednesday every year? ________________

3. Martin Luther King Jr. was born on January 15. But the holiday that honors his birthday comes on the third Monday in January. What is the date in 2014? ________________

4. Mr. Newman started tutoring Duke the second week in January. Duke was tutored every Tuesday and Thursday. Find the dates on the calendar.

________________ ________________

________________ ________________

________________ ________________

________________ ________________

5. Duke babysat for the Newmans every Saturday morning in January. On what dates in January did he work for them? Find the dates on the calendar.

________________ ________________

________________ ________________

contraction (con trac' shun)

Put together a word from List 1 and a word from List 2 to make a new word. Write the new word.

	List 1	List 2	New Word
1.	news	works	newspaper
2.	left	father	________
3.	fire	paper	________
4.	after	over	________
5.	air	ship	________
6.	room	noon	________
7.	grand	ever	________
8.	every	plane	________
9.	space	where	________
10.	for	mate	________

Underline the contraction in each sentence.
Write the two words from which the contraction is made.

Example: Math didn't interest Duke. did not

1. Aren't you still a student? ______ ______
2. What's the matter with school? ______ ______
3. I haven't passed a math test yet. ______ ______
4. I don't need math to run a press. ______ ______
5. I'll be your tutor. ______ ______
6. My family can't afford a tutor. ______ ______

Put *un-* at the beginning of each word to make another word. Write the word you make.

Example: furnished unfurnished

1. happy ____________________
2. interesting ____________________
3. safe ____________________
4. true ____________________
5. afraid ____________________

Fill in each blank with one of the words that starts with *un-*.

1. Math was ____________________ to Duke.
2. Duke was ____________________ in school.
3. That is an interesting story, but it is ____________________.
4. My nephew is ____________________ of the big waves.
5. It is ____________________ to be in the park at night.

Drop the ending from each word. Write the root word.

1. quitting ____________________
2. needed ____________________
3. dirty ____________________
4. classes ____________________
5. passing ____________________
6. countries ____________________
7. interested ____________________
8. placing ____________________
9. believed ____________________
10. studies ____________________

More Reading with *ū* and *oo*

music ū	cure u–e	argue ue	few ew
food oo	June u–e	blue ue	chew ew
student ū or oo	Duke u–e	Tuesday ue	news ew

Reading a Newspaper Story

page (paje)	board	lion (lī' un)
daily (dai' ly)	rope	headline (head' line)
climb (clīm)	cancer (can' ser)	president (prez' i dent)
group (groop)	winter (win' ter)	company (cum' pu ny)
wish	given (giv' en)	animal (an' i mul)
rate		

A daily newspaper in a city has many pages. Most people do not have time to read every story. Here are some ideas for reading your daily newspaper quickly.

Look at the first page of the paper. It has the main news stories of the day. Each story has a headline. The headline is in large print. The bigger the headline, the bigger the news story. The headlines can help you find the stories that you want to read.

Each news story tells five things. They are the Five *W*'s. They are *who, what, where, when,* and *why*. Look at the news story on this page. You can see where each of the Five *W*'s is.

where

when

what

who

why

Boy Gets Wish Before He Dies

Dallas, June 22—Pablo Lopez, a six-year-old boy, died today of cancer.

A few weeks before he died, he got his wish. His wish was to meet the President of the United States.

"My little boy had great courage," his father, Carlos Lopez, said. "He knew he had cancer. He wanted to live, but he was not afraid to die."

Last year, the little boy's right leg was removed to try to stop the cancer. But there was no cure for the kind of cancer he had.

Pablo told his father that he wanted to meet the President. His father made the boy's wish come true. The two of them went to Washington, D.C. There they met the President.

The President told Pablo, "Young man, you have great courage."

Use these ideas to read the newspaper on the next two pages. First, look at the headlines quickly. Then, as you read each news story, keep the Five *W*'s in mind.

HURON CITY, NEW YORK WEDNESDAY, JUNE 6, 2012

Huron City Daily News

Hearings Open on Utility Rates

The Valley Utility Company is asking the State Board of Public Utilities to let it raise its rates. If the state board agrees, the price of heat and lights will go up 15 per cent in October. Public hearings on this question began at 2:30 yesterday afternoon at the State Office Building.

At the hearing, Arthur Newman, president of the utility company, spoke first. He said, "The costs of running a utility company are going up. We have to pay more to workers. We need to make costly repairs and to buy new computers and other machines. We cannot continue to give today's services at today's rates."

More than 20 men and women from Huron United Citizens came to protest. The leader of that group, June Lewis, said, "The cost of heating homes must not go up this winter. The state must protect poor people. It must protect older people who are living on Social Security. If utility rates go up, they will not be able to afford both heat and food this winter."

Mike Romano spoke for a group of business leaders. He said, "High utility rates may make some businesses leave Huron City. New businesses will not come here when they can get cheaper rates in other cities."

The hearings will continue Thursday afternoon at 2:30 and will be open to the public.

Human Fly Rescued

Hoover City—The fire department rescued Mike O'Toole from high on the Union Building this morning. O'Toole, who says he is a human fly, was trying to climb the side of the building.

The Union Building, with 40 floors, is the highest building in this city. O'Toole had tried to climb it a few months ago. At that time, police told him not to try again. But O'Toole refused to listen.

O'Toole began his climb today at 7 a.m., before offices in the building were open. By 9:45, O'Toole was near the thirty-third floor, where he got stuck. He was not able to go up any higher, and he refused to go back below.

Traffic was tied up on the avenue below as people stopped to watch. When O'Toole got stuck, the people were amused. "Is he a human fly, or is he just stupid?" they asked.

O'Toole had been stuck for 20 minutes when the fire department came to his rescue. Fire fighters got a heavy rope from their fire truck. They carried the rope up to the thirty-fourth floor. There, they opened a window above O'Toole and threw the rope to him. O'Toole was able to climb the rope and go in the window.

After the fire fighters rescued O'Toole, police arrested him. "You can't stop me forever," O'Toole argued. "I haven't given up. I'll be back soon."

LIONS WILL HELP ZOO

"This city needs a better zoo," said Hugh Baker at the noon meeting of the Lions Club yesterday. Baker is the public information officer for the Huron City Zoo.

Baker said that the zoo is too cool for the animals in the winter. And the big animals don't have enough room to move freely. Too many lions have to live together.

"The lions don't look happy," Baker said. That got a big laugh from the Lions Club.

Baker said that the water animals need a bigger pool, and the birds need more room to fly.

Every week, more than 5,000 people go to the zoo, Baker reported. "On Sundays," he said, "there are so many people at the zoo that it's hard to see the animals."

Baker added, "The children keep telling me that they like the zoo a lot. Both the children and their parents learn a lot from the animals."

Baker ended by saying, "We need to think of the future for both the children and the animals. We need a better zoo."

The Lions Club agreed to raise $1,000 to help the lions in the zoo.

Tutors Honored

Parents and teachers of Valley View High School had a dinner Tuesday evening to honor a group of 20 tutors. These men and women have given much of their time this past year to help students in math and reading.

Dr. Mary Luther, president of the school board, was the main speaker of the evening. She thanked the tutors for their service.

"You have each helped a student in reading or math," she told the tutors. "But better than that, you have helped a student believe in himself."

Dr. Luther said that many high school students did better on state math and reading tests this year. She added that fewer students quit school.

Tutors will be needed for the next school year in math, reading, and English as a second language. Those who want to become tutors may get application forms from the school board office at 1385 Main Street.

Will of Music Star Made Public Today

The will of the late country music star Jimmy Lewis was made public today in Birmingham, Alabama.

Lewis left his shares in the Blue Star record company to his aunt Judy Jones, who raised him after his parents died. He left his home in Florida to his grandfather and grandmother, Mr. and Mrs. P. J. Lewis. He left $10,000 to each of his four nephews and nieces. To his cousin Luke Jones, who led Lewis's band, the young singer left his three sports cars.

Lewis died last year at the age of 27. A truck hit his car while he was driving to a Fourth of July concert in this city. Lewis grew up as a poor boy in Alabama. His music told of the hard life in the hills of Alabama and won him four gold records.

Jewels Stolen

The apartment of Mr. and Mrs. John Hoover of 1445 University Avenue was broken into late yesterday afternoon. Mrs. Hoover told police that a gold ring and her family jewels were missing from the bedroom. The Hoovers were not home at the time. But other people in the building remember seeing a man leaving the Hoovers' apartment. Police are looking for a young white man with red hair.

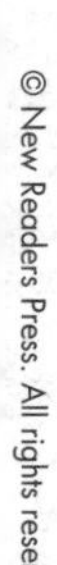

After you have read "Human Fly Rescued," answer these questions. Write short answers.

1. Who was rescued? ____________________

2. Where was he rescued? ____________________

3. When was he rescued? ____________________

4. What was he trying to do? ____________________

5. Why did he need to be rescued? ____________________

6. Who rescued him? ____________________

After you have read "Tutors Honored," answer these questions.

1. Who was honored? ____________________

2. Who honored them? ____________________

3. When were they honored? ____________________

4. What was given to honor them? ____________________

Practice

Say each word. Put the stress mark after the syllable that is stressed.

1. president	pres i dent
2. company	com pa ny
3. daily	dai ly
4. winter	win ter
5. avenue	av e nue
6. animal	an i mal
7. believe	be lieve

Make up three questions that ask *who, what, where, when,* or *why* for each of these stories:

Jewels Stolen

1. ______________________________

2. ______________________________

3. ______________________________

Lions Will Help Zoo

1. ______________________________

2. ______________________________

3. ______________________________

Add *-er* and *-est* to each word to make new words. Write the new words.

Example: poor ____poorer____ ____poorest____

1. rich ____________ ____________

2. cool ____________ ____________

3. dirty ____________ ____________

4. safe ____________ ____________

5. few ____________ ____________

6. new ____________ ____________

7. young ____________ ____________

8. funny ____________ ____________

uu

book = buuk

oo = uu

	cook	cook	cook
	hook	hook	hook
	brook	brook	brook
	foot	foot	foot
	good	good	good
	woods	woodz	woods

The Good Life in the Woods

Jake	Bush (Buush)	sugar (shuug' er)
plant	push (puush)	cabin (cab' in)
catch	pull (puul)	only (ōn' ly)
note	full (fuul)	notebook (note' buuk)
stove	took (tuuk)	understood (under stuud')
carve	could (cuud)	beautiful (bū' ti fuul)
	would (wuud)	

Sometimes a person knows a lot, but what he knows will die when he dies. With no relatives, friends, or students, he has no way of passing on what he knows to others.

The man in this story was that kind of person. Then someone wrote a book to share what that man knew. On the pages of a book, a person's ideas can live after him.

* * *

No one understood Jake Bush. No one understood why he wanted to live alone in the woods. At 83, Jake Bush was living alone in the north woods of New York State. He had lived there for 30 years.

Jake didn't care if people understood him or not. To him, life in the woods was good.

Jake Bush lived in a one-room cabin near a beautiful brook. The brook was full of fish. Jake could catch fish nearly every time he threw his hook into the water. He took fish home to cook every day. He took his drinking water from the brook, too.

The woods were full of wild plants. Jake cooked many kinds of these plants for food. He knew which plants were good to eat and which ones were not safe.

Jake cooked and heated his cabin with a wood-burning stove. He cut wood for his stove from dead trees. He cut up the big trees. Then he pushed and pulled the heavy pieces back to his cabin. He cut them into little pieces for his stove.

Jake Bush took good care of the woods where he lived. He never took more from the woods than he needed. He never tried to catch more fish than he could eat. He never threw trash into the brook.

In 30 years, Jake had never needed a doctor. He was hardly ever sick. Sometimes, he would catch cold or not feel very well. Then he cured himself with leaves and roots. Jake picked leaves and pulled up roots from wild plants. He used them to cure himself.

Jake had no radio or TV. He had only the music of the brook and the singing of the birds.

This was the life that Jake Bush was living when Sam Cook met him. Sam Cook was a writer who came to the north country to camp. Sam met Jake at the store.

Jake went to the store only a few times a year. He went there to buy coffee, sugar, fish hooks, and a few other things. There was only one way from Jake's home in the hills to the store. And that way was 15 miles each way on foot.

One day in June, Jake was in the store. He had some baskets and some animals carved from wood. The owner of the store would sell these things for him.

While the store owner was getting Jake's sugar and fish hooks, Sam Cook came up to Jake. "You're Mr. Bush, aren't you? I'm Sam Cook. I have been looking at the animals you carved. They're beautiful."

Jake looked up, but he didn't say anything.

"I would like to watch you carve something," Sam Cook said. "Would you let me watch?"

Jake said, "I live 15 miles from here. And you would have to go on foot."

"That's OK," Sam Cook said. "I'm camping on Stony Brook near Miller Hill. That's near your place, isn't it?"

"It's not too far," Jake said.

The two men left the store together. Sam carried a heavy bag of sugar for Jake. On the way, Sam told Jake that he was a writer. He said he would like to write a book on living in the woods.

"You had better live in the woods before you try to write a book," said Jake.

"I would like to," Sam said. "Would you let me camp near you for the next few months? I could learn some things by watching you."

"I can't stop you," Jake said. "I don't own the woods. But don't get in my way."

So Sam Cook moved his tent and sleeping bag to the woods near Jake's cabin. The first week, Jake hardly said anything in answer to Sam's questions. But, little by little, Jake grew to like the younger man. He let Sam help him cut trees and pull them back to his cabin. Jake pulled the heavy pieces of wood and Sam pushed. By pushing and pulling, they got the wood to the cabin.

Sam watched Jake do many things. As he watched, he took pictures, and he took notes in his notebook. Soon Sam's notebook was full of notes. Every night, Sam used his notes to work on his book.

One night, Sam read the first part of his book to Jake. "That's beautiful," Jake said. "I didn't think you understood why I love the woods. But from your book, I can tell that you love wild places and animals as much as I do."

"I have learned lots of things from you," said Sam. "And I hope to learn more. This book will pass on to others many of the things you know. But more than that, I hope the book will make people want to protect wild places like this."

"That idea is the main thing I want to pass on," said Jake.

Write *yes* if the sentence is true. Write *no* if it is not true.

__________ 1. Jake Bush had lived in the north woods for 30 years.

__________ 2. To Jake, life in the woods was good.

__________ 3. Jake heated his cabin with a wood-burning stove.

__________ 4. In the evenings, Jake watched TV.

__________ 5. When Jake was sick, he went to see a doctor.

__________ 6. Jake made baskets and carved animals from wood to sell.

__________ 7. Jake went to the store to buy things he could not make for himself.

__________ 8. Jake went to the store on his bicycle.

__________ 9. Sam Cook was a writer.

__________ 10. Jake asked Sam to stay with him in his cabin.

__________ 11. Jake liked the part of the book that Sam read to him.

__________ 12. A person's ideas can live after him on the pages of a book.

Write sentence answers to these questions.

1. What kind of book did Sam Cook want to write? ____________________

____

2. Why did Sam want to live near Jake for a few months? ____________________

____

____

____

3. What was the main thing that Jake wanted to pass on to others? ____________________

____

____

____

chapter (chap' ter)	contents (con' tents)	title (tī' tul)

Table of Contents

Here are the cover and the table of contents for the book that Sam Cook wrote. In the table of contents, you can find the title of each chapter in the book. You can find the page on which each chapter begins. The title of the book is on the cover.

Look at the table of contents and the book cover, and answer these questions. Write short answers.

1. What is the title of the book? ______________________________

2. Who wrote the book? ______________________________

3. What is the title of the first chapter? ______________________________

4. If you wanted to make baskets, which chapter would you read? ______________________________

   What page does it start on? ______________________________

5. Which two chapters would help you get your meals from the woods?

   ______________________________ and ______________________________

6. Which chapter tells ways to take care of the woods? ______________________________

   What page does it start on? ______________________________

Say the words. Circle the words with the sound *uu* as in *book*.

1. foot	food	noon	good
2. too	took	book	told
3. pull	pool	phone	full
4. soon	look	brook	hook
5. cook	cool	coat	could
6. wood	hook	hold	who
7. push	much	bush	put

Add the ending *-ful* to each root word. Write the new word in the blank.

Example: beauty ___beautiful___

1. hope ____________________
2. peace ____________________
3. thank ____________________
4. help ____________________
5. trust ____________________
6. care ____________________

Fill in each blank with one of the new words with *-ful*.

1. Jake's life in the woods was ____________________.
2. Sam was ____________________ that he could write a book on life in the woods.
3. Duke was ____________________ for Mr. Newman's help.
4. Be ____________________ when you swim in the lake.
5. Sam learned ways that he could be ____________________ to Jake.
6. At first, Jake was not ____________________ of Sam.

Put together a word from List 1 and a word from List 2 to make a new word. Write the new word.

	List 1	List 2	New Word
1.	under	book	understood
2.	home	stood	______
3.	note	times	______
4.	some	up	______
5.	head	mother	______
6.	pick	work	______
7.	grand	line	______
8.	him	one	______
9.	any	self	______

Would you like to live in the woods? Why or why not?

____

____

____

____

____

____

____

____

____

____

____

Lesson 9

	south	south	south
	house	hous	house
	shout	shout	shout
	ground	ground	ground
	mountain	moun' tin	mountain
1,000	thousand	thou' zand	thousand

Neighbors on the South Side

out	discuss (dis cus')
our	problem (prob' lem)
found	neighbor (nā' ber)
proud	neighborhood (nā' ber huud)
without (with out')	loan
about (u bout')	low (lōw)
around (u round')	housing (houz' ing)
council (coun' sil)	

Mountain City was a beautiful city. But not every part of Mountain City was beautiful. On the south side of the city, people had a lot of problems.

The south side was an old neighborhood. The houses there had been standing since about 1900. At one time, they had been fine houses. But as the city grew, people moved out of the south side. The people who stayed were mostly people without much money. Some were older people who had owned their homes for many years.

The neighborhood changed from a rich one to a poor one. But the taxes stayed high. Many owners of houses said they had no money for repairs after they paid taxes. Some owners even stopped paying taxes, and the city took over their houses. These empty houses had broken windows. Trash covered the ground around them, and the grass was not cut.

A hundred thousand people lived in Mountain City. About twenty thousand lived on the south side. The people on the south side did not like what was happening to their neighborhood. Some of them formed a group to do something about their problems. They named their group the South Side Neighbors.

The South Side Neighbors met every month to discuss their problems. They worked on one problem at a time. First, they found out the facts. Then, they discussed that problem with someone on the city council. One of the first problems they discussed was what to do about the empty houses.

A large group of South Side Neighbors went to a city council meeting. "When is the city going to do something about the empty houses next door to me?" asked one woman. "I have found some of our neighborhood children playing with matches there many times."

"There are a lot of houses like that around here," said the man next to her. "That's not safe for our neighborhood."

The city council said that it would board up the houses. But the south side people didn't want a lot of empty houses in their neighborhood, even if they were boarded up. "Don't board them up! Fix them up instead!" one man shouted. "It's not safe to go by an empty house on foot!"

"That's right!" another man shouted. "Our old people are afraid to go out!"

"That's true," said a woman. "Last month, my aunt was nearly killed on Maple Street. Two young men pushed her to the ground and pulled her into an empty house. They stole her money and told her not to open her mouth. But she tried to shout for help anyway, so they hit her in the mouth. Two of her teeth were broken, and she had to have ten stitches in her mouth. You must do something about those empty houses!"

The city council agreed to work on the problem. The council found out that the state had thousands of dollars for housing loans. Mountain City got some of that money. Then the city let people buy its old houses at a low cost. The city loaned money for repairs at a low cost. Other low-cost loans helped people pay for things that would save heat in the winter.

After much pushing by the South Side Neighbors, the city agreed to let older people pay lower taxes on their homes. And the city agreed to put in new sewers on the south side.

But the South Side Neighbors did not wait for the city to do everything. They found things they could do without much money. The group had clean-up days every month. Some people cleaned up trash and broken glass around the park. Others visited home owners and landlords and asked them to clean up the ground around their houses.

Some people formed a Neighborhood Watch. They took turns riding around the neighborhood at night. If anything looked funny, they reported it to the police. Everyone in the neighborhood felt safer.

After a few years, the south side was a cleaner, safer neighborhood. The South Side Neighbors were proud of their work. They were proud of their beautiful homes. They were proud of their clean parks and streets.

Story Checkup

Write two or three sentences to give the main ideas for each heading.

Problems of the south side of Mountain City

____

____

____

____

What the city agreed to do to help the south side

____

____

____

____

Ways the South Side Neighbors helped their neighborhood

____

____

____

____

east	fifth	St. (Street)	courthouse (court' house)
west	sixth	Ave. (Avenue)	

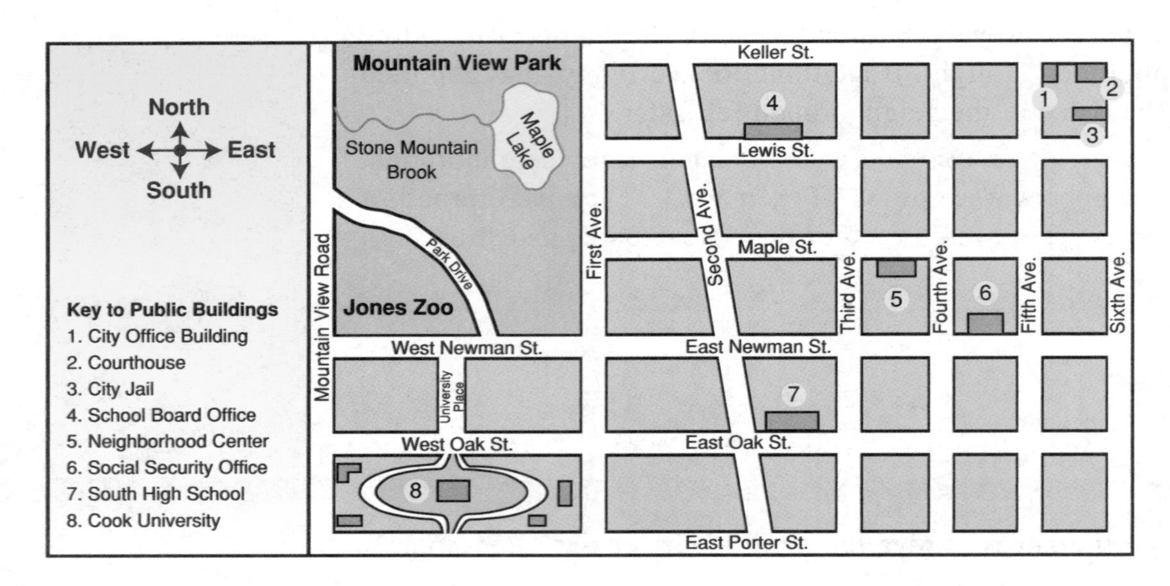

This is a map of the south side of Mountain City. Study the map and the key before answering the questions.

1. What does *St*. stand for? ______________________________
2. What does *Ave*. stand for? ______________________________
3. In this city, do the avenues run north and south or east and west? ______________
4. What school is on West Oak Street? ______________________________
5. What school is on East Oak Street? ______________________________
6. At what avenue does West Oak Street become East Oak Street? ______________
7. What public building is on Keller Street and Fifth Avenue? ______________
8. What public building is on Keller Street and Sixth Avenue? ______________
9. What building on Sixth Avenue is south of the courthouse? ______________
10. What street is on the north side of Jones Zoo? ______________________
11. To go from First Avenue to Sixth Avenue, do you go east or west? ______________
12. What street is the Neighborhood Center on? ______________________

Practice

In each line, circle the word that means the opposite of the first word.

1. in	an	on	out
2. low	big	high	little
3. south	cold	north	mouth
4. old	new	poor	child
5. full	little	empty	broken
6. good	beautiful	rude	bad
7. west	eats	east	fifth
8. with	without	about	around
9. push	carry	drop	pull

Homework

Add the ending *-ly* to each word. Write the new word in the blank.

1. most ____________________
2. proud ____________________
3. rude ____________________
4. day ____________________
5. month ____________________
6. safe ____________________
7. near ____________________
8. happy ____________________

Fill in each blank with one of the new words with *-ly*.

1. The South Side Neighbors held a meeting ____________________.
2. I like to read a ____________________ newspaper.
3. We cannot go out ____________________ at night.
4. The child is playing ____________________ by himself.
5. The people at the meeting were ____________________ from the south side.
6. After a few years, the people were able to speak ____________________ about their neighborhood.

ow = ou

town

ow = ou

	cow	cow	cow
	crowd	crowd	crowd
	down	down	down
	clown	clown	clown
	frown	frown	frown
	flower	flow′ er	flower

At the Howard County Fair

how	feet	summer (sum' er)
now	held	tractor (trac' ter)
Brown	pie	horse (hors)
Howard (How' erd)	win	sure (shuur)
Johnstown (Johns' town)	contest (con' test)	against (u genst')
Sue	county (coun' ty)	excite (ex site')
drove	easy (eaz' y)	unhappy (un hap' py)
fair	ribbon (rib' un)	

Mr. and Mrs. Ed Brown and their two teenagers were in town for the county fair. The Howard County Fair was held in Johnstown at the end of the summer. Every summer, crowds of people came to town for the fair. The week of the fair was the most exciting week of the year in Johnstown.

The Browns lived on a farm in Howard County. They had worked hard to get ready for the fair.

The Browns' son Tom hoped to win a blue ribbon for his cow Beauty. He had raised this cow from birth. Beauty gave more milk than any other cow on their farm. Tom was sure that she would win first prize.

Tom's sister Sue was excited about the horse show. Last year, she and her horse Sugar won a red ribbon for second prize. "I'm sure that Sugar is ready for a blue ribbon now," Sue told her brother.

Tom answered, "Yes, and Beauty is ready now, too."

At the fair, Sue found a place for Sugar in the horse barn. And Tom put Beauty in the cow barn.

Mrs. Brown took her flowers to the flower show. It was held in the morning. There were many kinds of flowers in the show. Mary Brown got a blue ribbon for her yellow roses. But the apple pie she took to the pie contest didn't win any prize.

In the afternoon, the family watched while Mr. Brown drove in the tractor-pulling contest. One by one, 20 farmers drove their big farm tractors. Each tractor was hooked up to the pulling contest machine. It was easy for the tractor to pull against the machine for the first few feet. Then, with each foot, it became harder and harder for the tractor to pull against the machine.

One farmer went 80 feet while his tractor was pulling against the machine. Another went 86 feet. Ed Brown went 92 feet with his tractor. He was the winner of the contest.

"Dad sure knows how to drive that tractor!" Tom shouted as his father got the blue ribbon.

The horse show was held later that afternoon, at 4:30. In one contest, the riders showed how well their horses followed orders. Sue was riding Sugar. Sugar stepped high. He turned and did other things that Sue ordered him to do. Some of the things that Sue and Sugar did were hard. But they did them so well that everything looked easy. When Sue got down from her horse's back, she was happy. Sugar had followed every one of her orders very well. She and Sugar won first prize.

When Tom showed his cow, Beauty won only third prize. Tom was unhappy that his cow didn't win first prize. He was frowning when his parents came up to him.

"You look unhappy, Son," his mother said. "Why are you frowning? Your prize is something to be proud of."

"That's easy for you to say!" Tom answered. "You won a blue ribbon. Now I'm the only person in the family who didn't win one."

"Don't speak to your mother like that," said Tom's father. "And don't be unhappy, Son. We are proud of you. You have made Beauty the best cow on our farm."

After their contests were over, Sue and Tom went on some exciting rides. One of the rides went up and down and around so fast that it made them yell.

Then they watched the clowns. One clown had a smile painted on his face. Another clown had a frown, and the corners of his mouth turned down. The clowns made the crowd laugh. Tom laughed, too. He was feeling happier.

That evening, a crowd of ten thousand people listened to the band. The Browns were in the crowd. Later, they watched the fireworks light up the dark night. "This is the best fair that Howard County has ever had, isn't it?" asked Mrs. Brown. Her family agreed that it was.

Story Checkup

alike (u like')

In what order did these things happen?
Put a number by each sentence to show the right order.

_____ After their contests, Sue and Tom went on rides and watched the clowns.

_____ Mr. Brown was the winner of the tractor-pulling contest.

_____ Mr. Brown told Tom that he was proud of him.

_____ When the Browns got to the fair, Sue and Tom put their animals in the barns.

_____ Later that afternoon, Sue and Sugar won a blue ribbon at the horse show.

_____ The Brown family watched the fireworks light up the dark night.

_____ Mrs. Brown won a blue ribbon at the flower show that morning.

_____ When Beauty won third prize, Tom was unhappy. He was the only one in his family who didn't win a blue ribbon.

Practice

Some words sound alike. But they are not written the same way, and they do not have the same meaning. Read the words that sound alike. Then write the right word in the blank.

Example:

(wood, would) Sam ___would___ like to watch Jake carve some animals from ___wood___.

(won, one) 1. Sue __________ a blue ribbon at the fair, but her brother did not win __________.

(eight, ate) 2. Last night, I __________ my dinner at __________ o'clock.

(to, too, two) 3. __________ sandwiches are __________ much for me __________ eat.

(new, knew) 4. Sam __________ that he would learn many __________ things from Jake.

million (mil' yun)

Reading Large Numbers

100	one hundred	250	two hundred fifty
1,000	one thousand	2,500	two thousand five hundred
10,000	ten thousand	25,000	twenty-five thousand
100,000	one hundred thousand	250,000	two hundred fifty thousand
1,000,000	one million	2,500,000	two million five hundred thousand

Write the numbers for these words.

a. two hundred ____________________

b. two thousand ____________________

c. twenty thousand ____________________

d. two hundred thousand ____________________

e. two million ____________________

Write the words for these numbers.

a. 750 ____

b. 7,500 ____

c. 75,000 ____

d. 750,000 ____

e. 7,500,000 ____

Say the words. Circle the words with the sound *ou* as in *south* and *town*.

1. slow down clown throw low
2. how now know show out
3. blow sound proud yellow flower
4. cow snow crowd below around
5. foot frown follow county council
6. found young house touch shout

Here are some more words that sound alike, but do not have the same meaning. Read the words that sound alike. Then write the right word in each blank.

(I, eye) 1. ____________ have something in my ____________.

(no, know) 2. ____________, I do not ____________ the answer.

(hear, here) 3. Come ____________ so that I can ____________ what you are saying.

(clothes, close) 4. Please ____________ the door when you change your ____________.

(right, write) 5. Did I ____________ the ____________ answer to the question?

(their, there) 6. Sue and Tom are over ____________ with ____________ parents.

Read the two words, and then write the contraction for them. The first contraction is filled in for you.

1. I am ___I'm___
2. we are ____________
3. is not ____________
4. are not ____________
5. do not ____________
6. did not ____________
7. have not ____________
8. that is ____________

More Reading with *ū, oo, uu,* and *ou*

music ū	cure u–e	argue ue	few ew
food oo	June u–e	blue ue	chew ew
student ū or oo	Duke u–e	Tuesday ue	news ew
book uu			
mouth ou	town ow		

1. Will Jake Have to Leave the Woods?

horseback (horse' back)	land	allow (u low')

When Sam Cook's book came out, the state found out that Jake Bush was living on state land. Jake lived on White Mountain in a huge state park.

Officers of the state parks department discussed what to do about Jake. "People are not allowed to live on state land," they said. "Mr. Bush will have to move."

One of the officers went on horseback to Jake's cabin in the woods. He told Jake what the parks department had said.

Jake frowned and said, "I have been living here for 30 years. Why are you telling me about this now?"

The officer answered, "A lot of people know about you now. If we allow you to stay here, everyone will want to live on free land."

Jake got angry. "I'm not moving!" he shouted. "If you want me out, you'll have to carry me out!"

After the officer left, Jake went to the store on foot. There he phoned Sam Cook and told him the bad news. "I'll do my best to help you," Sam said. "I'll tell the newspapers."

Soon the newspapers were full of stories about Jake's problem. People who had read the book about Jake came to his rescue. They understood why Jake loved the woods. They didn't want the state to push him out. Thousands of people wrote letters to protest. Crowds marched in the state capital.

The parks department held another meeting. When it was over, one of the officers spoke to news reporters. He said, "We understand that Mr. Bush knows a lot about the woods and wild animals. If he will take good care of them for us, we will allow him to stay in his home. He can get a permit to live on state land in the park."

Sam Cook took the news to Jake. "Will you agree to this plan?" he asked the old man.

"I sure will!" said Jake. "It's just what I wanted."

2. Running for Office

Gladys (Glad' us)	should (shuud)

Gladys Brooks lived on the south side of Mountain City. She was raising her five children alone, and she didn't have much money. But she found time to work with the South Side Neighbors on housing problems. Gladys became a leader in that group. She got people to work together. And she learned how to speak in public.

Her friends told her, "No one on the city council knows what our life is like. They have never been poor. They have never been out of work for months and months. You should run for city council. You could speak for us."

"I'll have to think about it," Gladys said. She discussed the idea with many people. Everyone told her, "You should run for office."

Gladys made up her mind. "I'll run," she told the South Side Neighbors. "But I can't win without your help."

The South Side Neighbors went from house to house in their neighborhood. They told everyone what a good leader Gladys Brooks was. "You should vote for her," they said.

Gladys Brooks spoke to many groups on the south side. She told them what she would do on the city council. "We need more jobs and child care centers for working parents. We need low-cost housing and better schools. We need to make our streets safe. I will work hard to make the south side a better place to live."

When the people of Mountain City voted, Gladys Brooks won a place on the city council. The South Side Neighbors were proud of her. They gave her a party.

"Thank you for helping me to win," Gladys told them. "But our work has just started. We must work together for a better south side and for a better city."

3. Changes on the Farm

Brunoski (Broo nos' kē)	power (pow' er)
electric (e lec' tric)	plow

The Browns' farm had been in the family for 100 years. Ed Brown's grandfather, Joe Brunoski, came to America when he was 18 years old. When Joe came into the country, his name was changed from Brunoski to Brown. At first, Joe Brown worked on another man's farm. In time, he was able to get married and buy a farm in Howard County.

The farm land was good, but the house was old. Mrs. Brown was unhappy until she planted flowers around the house to make it more beautiful.

For many years, Joe and his wife Molly had to do everything by hand. There was no electric power. They had no electric lights or electric stove. Molly cooked on a wood-burning stove. Joe and Molly had to milk their cows by hand. Joe plowed the hard ground with a team of horses. The horses pulled the plow. On Saturdays, Joe and Molly drove the horses into town.

The Browns got a telephone and a radio sometime in the 1920s. The family was even more excited when they got their first car in the 1930s. With the car, they could go into Johnstown quickly.

When the Browns' oldest son, Jim, started to run the farm in the 1940s, he got a bank loan. With the loan, he got a tractor to pull the plow. About the same time, the county put in electric power. At last, the Browns had electric power for lights, heat, and cooking. With the electric power, they could use milking machines to milk the cows. By the 1950s, the Browns had running water in their house.

Jim Brown let his youngest son, Ed, take over the farm in the 1970s. Ed got bank loans to build a new house and buy more farm machines. Ed Brown is thinking of changing the family name back to Brunoski. He is proud of the farm that his grandfather started.

The Brown farm is like many family farms in America. Over the years, many changes have come to America's farms. Farmers now have machines, electric power, and even computers to help them. But they still work hard from the time the sun comes up until the sun goes down.

Story Checkup

Write two questions about each story. Use the question words *why, how,* and *when.*

Story 1: Will Jake Have to Leave the Woods?

1. ______________________________

2. ______________________________

Story 2: Running for Office

1. ______________________________

2. ______________________________

Story 3: Changes on the Farm

1. ______________________________

2. ______________________________

Practice

In each line, circle the word that means the opposite of the first word.

1. up	out	down	about
2. winter	cold	hot	summer
3. happy	angry	unhappy	glad
4. beginning	end	first	third
5. first	best	blue	last
6. easy	sure	hard	proud
7. leave	catch	discuss	stay
8. head	foot	hand	mouth

plural (pluur' ul), loaves (loavz), tooth, vowel (vow' ul)

Read each word. Then write the word in its plural form.

Example: loaf loaves

1. foot ____________
2. tooth ____________
3. man ____________
4. woman ____________
5. child ____________
6. wife ____________
7. leaf ____________
8. loaf ____________

Fill in each blank with one of the words in the plural form. (You may use the example word in your answers.)

1. A maple tree has pretty ____________.
2. It is not safe for ____________ to play with matches.
3. Workers may bring their husbands and ____________ to the company picnic.
4. Two men and three ____________ are on the city council.
5. I had two ____________ pulled last week.
6. Get two ____________ of bread when you go to the store.
7. That mountain is about twenty thousand ____________ high.
8. There are more women than ____________ over the age of 75.

In each line, circle the word with the same vowel sound as the first word.

1. book	too	cook	town
2. south	tooth	shout	soon
3. chew	snow	foot	threw
4. blue	true	blow	brook
5. town	took	clown	June
6. pool	pull	stole	school
7. music	argue	mouth	woods

lawn

aw

	saw	saw	saw
	law	law	law
	claw	claw	claw
	crawl	crawl	crawl
	awful	aw' fuul	awful
	Dawson	Daw' son	Dawson

1. The Neighbors' Dog

dog	Shaw	bark	fence (fens)
watchdog (watch' dog)	long	dig	Jerry (Jerr' y)
across (u cross')	strong	hole	sorry (sorr' y)

Jerry Dawson had a beautiful lawn. His neighbors, the Shaws, had a big, strong dog. Their dog liked to dig holes with his long claws.

One Saturday morning, Jerry Dawson was cutting his lawn. He saw a big hole in the lawn near the fence. Jerry Dawson shouted across the fence to Bob Shaw. "Your dog has made an awful hole in my lawn again. He crawled under the fence. I can see his claw marks."

Bob Shaw came to the fence. He saw why Jerry Dawson was so angry. "I'm awfully sorry," Bob said. "But what can I do? He's a strong dog. He can dig a hole under my fence with his long claws."

"Being sorry isn't good enough," said Jerry. "Tie him up. That's the law. You know the law of this town as well as I do. It's against the law to let a dog run free."

"I don't let my dog run free on the streets," said Bob. "The law says a dog doesn't have to be tied up if you have a fence around your land. I don't want to tie my dog up. I need him as a watchdog."

"I'm sorry, but this has been going on long enough," said Jerry. "You'll have to fix the fence so your dog can't crawl under it. He had better not dig any more holes in my lawn, or I'll report you to the police!" By that time, Bob was awfully angry, too. Both men were shouting across the fence.

A few nights later, the sound of a dog barking woke Jerry up. The Shaw's dog was barking and barking. Jerry crawled out of bed and looked out the window. Just then, the lights came on in Bob's house. Both men saw someone running across Jerry's lawn and down the street.

Bob helped Jerry check his house. In the kitchen, they found a broken window. "Your dog is a good watchdog. I'm glad to have him as a neighbor," Jerry said. "But I still don't want him digging holes in my lawn. I'll help you make the fence stronger."

au = aw

Paul
au

	haul	haul	haul
	sauce	saus	sauce
	laundry	laun′ dry	laundry
	cause	cauz	cause
	because	bē cauz′	because
	automobile	au′ tō mō bēl	automobile

2. An Accident in the Fog

fault	wet	front (frunt)	couldn't (could' unt)
fog	along (u long')	accident (ac' si dent)	highway (high' way)
off	exit (ex' it)	tomato (tu mā' tō)	

When Paul Jones came in the door, his wife cried out, "What happened?" Her husband was covered with something red and wet.

"It's only tomato sauce," Paul said. Then he told her what had happened.

That morning, Paul was driving a laundry truck along the highway. He was hauling clean laundry into the city. Paul was not driving fast. He had never had an accident in 15 years of driving trucks. But he was afraid of having one now.

It had stopped raining, but the highway was still wet. Fog covered everything. Because of the heavy fog, Paul could hardly see the road in front of him. Behind him was a huge truck. It was hauling big cans of tomato sauce. Paul could see the lights of the truck. But because of the fog, he couldn't tell how big it was.

There was a light gray automobile moving along next to Paul. But Paul couldn't see it because of the fog. The automobile's lights were off.

Paul was nearly at the exit where he wanted to turn off the highway. He was watching for the exit sign. It was hard to see the exit sign in the fog. Just then, the gray car cut in front of Paul's truck and slowed down for the exit.

Paul didn't see the automobile. His truck ran into it. Because the road was wet, the huge truck behind Paul couldn't stop in time. When the driver tried to turn out of the way, his truck went off the highway and turned over. The tomato sauce he was hauling went everywhere.

When the police came, it looked like the three drivers were badly hurt. But they were just covered with tomato sauce.

The police tried to find out what caused the accident. They asked each driver how it happened. Paul and the other truck driver said that it was not their fault. The police agreed.

The police said that the fog and the wet road were two of the causes. But the main cause was the driver of the automobile. "This accident was your fault," they told him. "You should not have been driving in the fog with your lights off. And you should not have cut in front of the truck."

Paul finished his story. "I'm sorry I had my first accident," he told his wife. "But I'm glad no one was hurt, and I'm glad I wasn't at fault." As he pulled off his clothes, Paul added, "Now I have to do some laundry of my own."

Finish each sentence.

Story 1: The Neighbor's Dog

1. Jerry Dawson was angry with Bob Shaw because ______________________________

____

2. Bob Shaw was angry with Jerry Dawson because ______________________________

____

3. Bob Shaw didn't want to tie up his dog because ______________________________

____

4. One night, Jerry woke up because ______________________________

____

5. After that, Jerry was glad to have the dog as a neighbor because ______________________________

____

Story 2: An Accident in the Fog

1. Paul Jones was driving a truck along the highway because ______________________________

____

2. Paul could hardly see the road in front of him because ______________________________

____

3. The driver of the big truck couldn't stop in time because ______________________________

____

4. The police said the driver of the gray automobile was at fault because ______________________________

____

____

5. Paul's wife cried out when she saw him because ______________________________

____

Getting Accident Information

auto	rear	no. (number)
Ford	complete (com plete')	Ohio (ō hī' ō)
insurance (in shuur' uns)	damage (dam' ij)	

If you have an auto accident, your insurance company will help you complete an accident report. But you will need to find out some information at the time of the accident. The form below will help you remember what to find out. Complete the form, using these facts.

At 7:30 this morning, your car was hit from the rear by a brown 2008 Ford car, with Ohio license plates, number XCL 140. Your car was damaged in the rear and has a broken rear window. Peter Smith, of 500 Center St., River Town, Ohio 44433, was driving the Ford. His insurance company is National Auto Insurance. His Ford was not damaged. Jim Parker, of 140 Main St. in your city, saw the accident, which took place at the corner of Oak St. and Second Ave. in your city. No one was hurt.

Other driver's name and address ______________________________

____

Other driver's license plate no. ____________________ State __________

Other driver's automobile: Make __________ Year __________ Color __________

Other driver's insurance company ______________________________

Place of accident: City ____________________ State __________

Streets ______________________________

Date of accident ____________________ Time of accident ______ a.m. ______ p.m.

Damage to other automobile ______________________________

Damage to my automobile ______________________________

Name and address of any person who saw the accident ______________________________

____

Circle the words with the sound *aw* as in *lawn* and *Paul.*

1. saw	snow	claw	car
2. low	law	look	new
3. pull	hurt	haul	awful
4. crawl	rule	paw	cook
5. Shaw	fault	smell	sauce
6. cause	laugh	haul	auto

Add *-er* and *-est* to each root word to make new words.
Write the new words by the root word.
Then fill in each blank in the sentences with the right word.

1. wet ____________________ ____________________

Mr. Brown says that this summer is ____________________ than last summer.

He says it is the ____________________ summer he remembers.

2. strong ____________________ ____________________

Jerry, Paul, and Lewis had a contest to see which one was ____________________.

Jerry was ____________________ than Paul.

But Lewis was the ____________________ of the three men.

3. long ____________________ ____________________

Hugh's boat is 12 feet long. Ed's boat is 14 feet long. Bob's boat is 16 feet long.

Ed's boat is ____________________ than Hugh's.

Bob's boat is ____________________ than Ed's.

Bob's boat is the ____________________ of the three boats.

In each line, circle the word that is the opposite of the first word.

1. wet	cold	hot	dry
2. light	dark	bright	brown
3. front	top	back	before
4. long	little	short	high
5. over	under	before	into
6. off	in	out	on
7. sorry	angry	sad	glad
8. rear	next	front	side
9. before	after	soon	along

Say each word. Put the stress mark after the syllable that is stressed.

1. because	be cause
2. automobile	au to mo bile
3. accident	ac ci dent
4. laundry	laun dry
5. across	a cross
6. damage	dam age
7. tomato	to ma to
8. sorry	sor ry
9. unhappy	un hap py
10. excite	ex cite
11. insurance	in sur ance
12. complete	com plete

all = awl

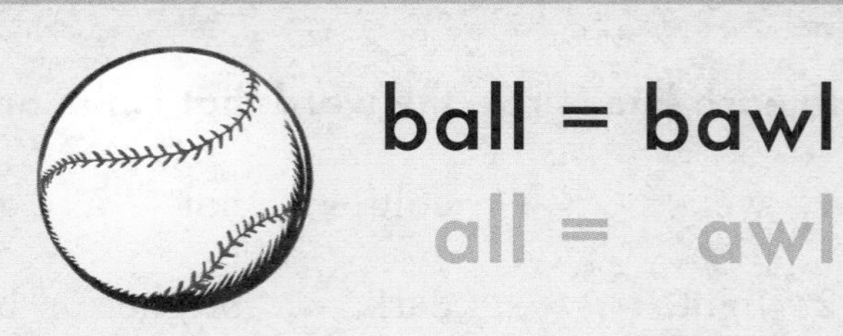

	wall	wall	wall
	hall	hall	hall
	fall	fall	fall
	call	call	call
	small	small	small
	baseball	base' ball	baseball

Jackie Robinson

Jackie (Jack' ē)	fame	series (sēr' ēz)
Robinson (Rob' in son)	fan	basketball (bas' ket ball)
Brooklyn (Brook' lin)	kept	football (foot' ball)
Dodgers (Doj' erz)	Branch	California (Cal i forn' yu)
national (nash' un ul)	Rickey (Rick' ey)	manager (man' ij er)
league (leag)	also (awl' sō)	prejudice (prej' uu dis)
crack	chance (chans)	talk (tawk)
track	major (mā' jer)	

Crack! At the crack of the bat, the ball went flying over the wall. A home run for Jackie Robinson! The crowd was excited. Fans yelled for Jackie and the Brooklyn Dodgers.

The year was 1947. That fall, the Brooklyn Dodgers were the top baseball team in the National League. Jackie Robinson was voted the best new player of the year. He was also the first black player in the major leagues.

Until 1947, all the baseball players in the major leagues were white. A wall of prejudice kept black players out. There were many good black players and some great ones. But they weren't allowed to play in the major leagues. Blacks had to play in smaller black leagues.

Branch Rickey, the president and manager of the Brooklyn Dodgers, had the courage to go against the all-white rule. He believed that any player, black or white, should have the chance to play in the major leagues.

Branch Rickey looked for a black player for his Brooklyn Dodgers. He knew that many fans would not like having a black player on the team. The fans would call him names. Some Dodger players would refuse to talk to him. Some teams would refuse to play the Dodgers. It would take a very strong man to stand up to this prejudice. He would also have to be a very good player.

Rickey picked Jackie Robinson. Jackie was born in the South in 1919. When he was small, his mother moved to California with her five children. Jackie went to high school and college in California.

Jackie became a sports star in high school. He played basketball, football, and baseball. He was also a track star. Then he went to a small two-year college, where he continued to be a sports star. His record in sports gave him a chance to go to the University of California. There, he was the first student to win a letter in all four sports—football, basketball, baseball, and track.

When Jackie's mother got sick, he dropped out of college and went to work. Then he went into the armed services. When he got out, he played ball for one of the black teams. That was where the manager of the Dodgers found him.

Branch Rickey talked with Jackie Robinson. The manager said it would be hard to play with the Dodgers. The first black player would have to stand up to prejudice without fighting back. "Do you think you can do that?" Rickey asked.

"I have been fighting prejudice all my life," said Jackie. "This is a chance to do it by playing ball."

That first year was hard. Fans called Robinson names. Players on other teams called him names. Some players threw the baseball to hit him. Jackie did not fight back. He just kept on playing the best he could.

Jackie played so well that the fans began to like him. The team liked him, too. The wall of prejudice began to fall. After three years, Rickey agreed that Robinson could talk back if anyone called him a name.

Jackie played with the Dodgers for 10 years. He played in six World Series. He led the Dodgers to win the Series in 1955. That was a great time in Jackie's life. Another came in 1962 when he was voted into the National Baseball Hall of Fame.

Jackie Robinson was the first black voted into baseball's Hall of Fame. He was voted into the Hall of Fame because he was a great all-around baseball player. He didn't get that honor because he was the first black player in the major leagues. But he is remembered mainly for that. Jackie Robinson opened the doors for other black players in major league baseball.

Story Checkup

Write sentence answers to each of these questions.

1. What kind of black player did Branch Rickey want for the Brooklyn Dodgers?

___

___

2. Why was the first year as a player on the Brooklyn Dodgers hard for Jackie?

___

___

3. Why was Jackie Robinson voted into the National Baseball Hall of Fame?

___

___

spring	December (Dē sem' ber)
February (Feb' roo ār y)	Thanksgiving (Thanks giv' ing)
August (Au' gust)	Christmas (Cris' mus)
September (Sep tem' ber)	season (sea' zun)
November (Nō vem' ber)	

CALENDAR FOR THE YEAR 2016

JANUARY

S	M	T	W	T	F	S
					1	2
3	4	5	6	7	8	9
10	11	12	13	14	15	16
17	18	19	20	21	22	23
24	25	26	27	28	29	30
31						

FEBRUARY

S	M	T	W	T	F	S
	1	2	3	4	5	6
7	8	9	10	11	12	13
14	15	16	17	18	19	20
21	22	23	24	25	26	27
28	29					

MARCH

S	M	T	W	T	F	S
		1	2	3	4	5
6	7	8	9	10	11	12
13	14	15	16	17	18	19
20	21	22	23	24	25	26
27	28	29	30	31		

APRIL

S	M	T	W	T	F	S
					1	2
3	4	5	6	7	8	9
10	11	12	13	14	15	16
17	18	19	20	21	22	23
24	25	26	27	28	29	30

MAY

S	M	T	W	T	F	S
1	2	3	4	5	6	7
8	9	10	11	12	13	14
15	16	17	18	19	20	21
22	23	24	25	26	27	28
29	30	31				

JUNE

S	M	T	W	T	F	S
			1	2	3	4
5	6	7	8	9	10	11
12	13	14	15	16	17	18
19	20	21	22	23	24	25
26	27	28	29	30		

JULY

S	M	T	W	T	F	S
					1	2
3	4	5	6	7	8	9
10	11	12	13	14	15	16
17	18	19	20	21	22	23
24	25	26	27	28	29	30
31						

AUGUST

S	M	T	W	T	F	S
	1	2	3	4	5	6
7	8	9	10	11	12	13
14	15	16	17	18	19	20
21	22	23	24	25	26	27
28	29	30	31			

SEPTEMBER

S	M	T	W	T	F	S
				1	2	3
4	5	6	7	8	9	10
11	12	13	14	15	16	17
18	19	20	21	22	23	24
25	26	27	28	29	30	

OCTOBER

S	M	T	W	T	F	S
						1
2	3	4	5	6	7	8
9	10	11	12	13	14	15
16	17	18	19	20	21	22
23	24	25	26	27	28	29
30	31					

NOVEMBER

S	M	T	W	T	F	S
		1	2	3	4	5
6	7	8	9	10	11	12
13	14	15	16	17	18	19
20	21	22	23	24	25	26
27	28	29	30			

DECEMBER

S	M	T	W	T	F	S
				1	2	3
4	5	6	7	8	9	10
11	12	13	14	15	16	17
18	19	20	21	22	23	24
25	26	27	28	29	30	31

Dates to remember

January 1	New Year's Day
January 18	Birthday of Martin Luther King Jr.
February 15	Presidents Day
March 20	First day of spring
June 14	Flag Day
June 20	First day of summer
July 1	Canada Day
July 4	Fourth of July
September 5	Labor Day
September 22	First day of fall
October 10	Thanksgiving Day in Canada
November 24	Thanksgiving Day in United States
December 21	First day of winter
December 25	Christmas

On the calendar, circle each date in the list.
Then write short answers to these questions.

1. On what day of the week does Christmas come in 2016? ____________________
2. What holiday falls on the third Monday in February? ____________________
3. Which country has its Thanksgiving Day in November? ____________________
4. Are there any holidays in August? ____________________
5. When does each season begin? Write the dates.

   Spring: ____________________ Summer: ____________________

   Fall: ____________________ Winter: ____________________
6. Which season does August come in, spring or summer? ____________________
7. What holiday comes in September? ____________________
8. Which month does Christmas come in, November or December? ____________________

Write the right word in the blank.

(clowns, claws, clean) 1. The cat hurt the baby with its ____________________.

(lawn, law, lake) 2. Jerry cut his ____________________ every week.

(holes, hauls, halls) 3. Paul ____________________ laundry in his truck.

(laws, low, paws) 4. We should know the ____________________ of our country.

(well, wall, fall) 5. The ball went flying over the ____________________.

(smile, small, smell) 6. Jackie moved to California when he was ____________________.

Each of these words has two or more meanings.
Write sentences to show two meanings for each word.

Example: right 1. I write with my right hand.

2. I wrote the right word in the blank.

fall 1. ____

2. ____

star 1. ____

2. ____

fair 1. ____

2. ____

left 1. ____

2. ____

false (fawls), compound (com' pound)

Write *True* if the sentence is true. Write *False* if the sentence is false.

__________ 1. Jackie Robinson was born in California.

__________ 2. Jackie became a sports star in high school.

__________ 3. Until 1950, all the baseball players in the major leagues were white.

__________ 4. Branch Rickey believed that only white players should play in the major leagues.

__________ 5. In 1947, Jackie Robinson was voted the best new player of the year.

__________ 6. When fans called Jackie names, he refused to play.

__________ 7. Jackie Robinson played with the Dodgers for 10 years.

__________ 8. Jackie Robinson was voted into baseball's Hall of Fame because he was the first black player in the major leagues.

Put together a word from List 1 and a word from List 2 to make a new word. Write the compound word. (You may use words in List 2 more than one time.)

	List 1	List 2	Compound Word
1.	base	father	__________
2.	foot	back	__________
3.	high	ball	__________
4.	watch	way	__________
5.	basket	paper	__________
6.	left	dog	__________
7.	news	over	__________
8.	horse		__________
9.	grand		__________

caught = caut
aught = aut

aught = aut
ought = aut

bought = baut
ought = aut

	taught	taught	taught
	daughter	daugh' ter	daughter
	fought	fought	fought
	thought	thought	thought
	brought	brought	brought

Between Two Worlds

American (U mār' i can)	desk	often (awf' en)
classroom (class' room)	walk (wawk)	pencil (pen' sil)
grandchildren (grand' children)	war (wor)	ticket (tick' et)
Tran Ty Lan (Tran Tī Lan)	Wong	trouble (trub' ul)
Vietnam (Vē et nom')	between (bē tween')	

Tran Ty Lan found a desk in the classroom and sat down. She took out the new pencils she had bought. "It feels good to sit down," Lan thought as she put her pencils on her desk.

As Tran Ty Lan waited for her night class to begin, she thought about her job at the nursing home. She was tired from working there all day. But she liked taking food to the old people. She liked listening to them talk and doing things to make them feel better. "But I don't understand American ways," Lan thought. "In Vietnam, old people are not put in nursing homes. Grandmothers and grandfathers live with their children and grandchildren. Children are taught to take care of their parents when their parents get old."

Lan thought about her own parents, her brother, her two daughters, and her cousin. They were all living together in a small apartment in New York.

Then Lan thought about Vietnam. Her husband had fought in the war and died. Her father-in-law was dead, too, but he had not fought in the war. After the war, rats brought sickness to the city. Her father-in-law had caught the sickness and died. Now Lan was trying to help her mother-in-law in Vietnam. Every month, she bought sugar, pencils, clothes, and other things to send to her mother-in-law.

The other students began to arrive for class. Molly Hall sat at the desk next to Lan's. Molly and Lan often sat together. Molly's husband had fought and died in the Vietnam War, too. But Molly had married again. "My children

needed a father," Molly often told Lan. "Your children need a father, too. And you, Lan, don't you want to marry again?"

When Molly spoke this way, Lan told her, "You are American. In Vietnam, we are taught that a good daughter marries only one time." But Lan was beginning to think that Molly's idea was not so bad. On TV, Lan saw that many American women married a second time.

Just as Molly sat down, Tom Wong walked into the classroom. Tom taught the math class in night school. He had lived in America all his life; his grandfather had come to America from China. "Now there's the man for you," Molly told Lan. "He's handsome and kind. And I think he likes you. He looks at you often when he's teaching."

After class, Lan started walking to the bus stop. "Want a ride?" she heard. Lan jumped at the sound of Tom Wong's words. "It's too much trouble for you," she said.

"No trouble at all," Tom said. "Come on. It's late, and this neighborhood isn't very safe at night." Lan got into the car. She wondered what her mother and father would think.

Lan's father saw the car stop in front of the apartment. He saw Tom Wong get out and open the car door for his daughter. He saw the man walk her to the door, talk to her, and smile.

When Lan came in, her mother asked, "Daughter, who brought you home?"

"My teacher brought me," Lan said.

"I hope he is only your teacher and not also your boyfriend," said her mother.

Two days later, Lan got a phone call from her aunt in Canada. "Your daughters need all of your love," she told Lan. "You ought to think of their needs and their future. If you have a boyfriend, you will not give as much time to them. If you marry again, your new husband may not love your children. I see trouble for them."

Lan's brother told her, "Mother and Father have been calling and writing to our relatives. Mother and Father are afraid. If you marry again, our people will talk. They will say you do not care about your children and your family. You ought to think of us. You ought to think of our relatives in Vietnam."

Then Lan got letters from Vietnam. Her mother-in-law asked, "How are my grandchildren? Do they remember me? Do you tell them about their father? Remember what you were taught as a child, and teach them the ways of our country."

Lan's sister-in-law wrote from Vietnam, "I hope you don't marry again. We love you. Don't forget us."

One day, Tom Wong stopped by the apartment. "Look what I caught!" he said. "I thought your family would like some fresh fish."

When Lan saw Tom, her heart jumped. She smiled. "Thank you," she said. "Come in."

Tom talked to Lan's father and mother. "You have a fine daughter," he said. "She's a good student." Lan's father smiled and thanked Tom.

Two days later, Lan's father bought three bus tickets. He told his daughter, "These tickets are for you and your children. You are going to California to live with your cousin there." He went on, "I am thinking of your children and your husband's family. Give all of your love to them. It will be better that way."

Tran Ty Lan took the tickets. She took her daughters to California as her father told her to. On the bus, Lan had much time to think. She thought about her family and the old ways of Vietnam. She thought about her new friends Molly and Tom and their American ways. "I feel caught between Vietnam and America," she thought. "I feel caught between old ways and new."

Answer each question in one or two sentences.

1. Why did Lan question the idea of putting old people in nursing homes?

____

____

2. Why didn't Lan's family want her to marry again?

____

____

3. Why was Lan beginning to think that marrying again was not a bad idea?

____

____

Write *True* if the sentence is true. Write *False* if the sentence is false.

__________ 1. Lan's husband had fought in the war in Vietnam.

__________ 2. Lan's mother-in-law lived in Canada.

__________ 3. Lan's family wanted her to marry again.

__________ 4. Lan's friend Molly was an American.

__________ 5. Tom Wong was born in China.

__________ 6. Tom Wong brought Lan's family some fish.

__________ 7. Lan refused to go to California to live.

__________ 8. Lan felt caught between two worlds.

156 Park Street
Roberts, California 95102
June 15, 1984

Dear Molly,

Are you wondering what happened to me? My daughters and I moved to California to live with my cousin. My father thought it would be best for me to leave New York.

I'm sorry I could not talk with you before I left. You are a very good friend. I will never forget you.

You helped me understand this new land. I hope I helped you understand the ways of my people and why a daughter must follow her father's wishes.

I miss school and Tom Wong. I want to explain American ways and my feelings about Tom to my parents. I want to become more American, but I want to keep the ways of Vietnam, too. I want to change, but change is very hard.

I hope we will continue to be friends. Please write to me.

Your friend,
Lan

Practice

Add the ending *-ness* to each root word. Write the new word in the blank.

Examples: sick sickness lovely loveliness

1. kind ____________________
2. sad ____________________
3. quiet ____________________
4. happy ____________________

Fill in each blank with one of the new words with *-ness*.

1. Lan's life was filled with ____________________ when her husband died.
2. Lan thanked Molly for her ____________________.
3. My friend's grandchildren are her greatest ____________________.
4. Jake likes the ____________________ of the woods.

Homework

Circle the words with the sound *aw* as in *law, Paul, ball, taught, bought.*

1. caught could cute bought
2. night thought fall throw
3. teach right small taught
4. laugh daughter walk trouble
5. false fought fight football

Answer with two or three sentences.

Why did Tran Ty Lan feel caught between two worlds? ____

____

____

____

	toy	toy	toy
	annoy	u noy′	annoy
	enjoy	en joy′	enjoy
	employ	em ploy′	employ
	employee	em ploy′ ee	employee
	destroy	dē stroy′	destroy

oi = oy

oil
oi

	coin	coin	coin
	join	join	join
	point	point	point
	noise	noiz	noise
	voice	vois	voice
	avoid	u void'	avoid

The Year I Was Unemployed

Roy	wrong (rong)	downtown (down' town')
laid	I've	hopeless (hope' less)
less	they'll	Johnson (John' son)
might	almost (awl' mōst)	employment (employ' ment)
slept	always (awl' wayz)	unemployment (un employ' ment)
Joyce (Joys)	worry (wur' y)	unemployed (un employed')
shook (shuuk)	support (su port')	disappoint (dis u point')
truth (trooth)		

I'll never forget the year I was out of work. That year almost destroyed me. It almost destroyed my family, too.

My name is Roy Johnson. I was 36 that year. I had been employed at a small factory for almost 10 years. My job was to take care of the machines. I cleaned and oiled them. I often repaired them when they broke down. I enjoyed my job, and I liked my employer.

But that year, business started slowing down. The company had less work. At first, only the newest employees were laid off. I was one of the last employees who got laid off.

For three weeks, I avoided telling my wife Joyce the truth. Every morning, I left the house and went out to look for work. Then one day, Joyce tried to phone me at work. My older boy, Jimmy, had been hurt at school. My employer told Joyce that I had been laid off.

That news almost destroyed my wife. She was disappointed in me. She felt that I didn't trust her enough to tell her the truth. It wasn't that. I didn't want to worry her. I thought I might be able to find another job soon. I asked Joyce not to tell our boys. I didn't want them to worry.

I was reading the employment ads in the paper every day. There were not many ads for jobs I could do. I went to the state employment office. I thought I might get some help there. The employment office did send me to a lot of companies. But everywhere I went, I always got the same answer, "Leave an application." A lot of other people were unemployed that year. At some companies, they had boxes of applications that people had left.

I was able to get unemployment insurance. And my wife was working part time. With her pay and my unemployment insurance, we were able to get by. But it wasn't easy.

Weeks went by, and then months. It wasn't as easy to find another job as I had thought. After a while, I gave up trying so hard. I was sure that my wife was disappointed in me. So I began to avoid her and the boys. Many times, I didn't join them for meals. Often, I stayed out late drinking beer. Some days, I stayed in bed and slept all day.

Little things began to annoy me. My wife's voice annoyed me when she asked, "Where did you look today?" The noise she made cleaning house annoyed me. My children's voices annoyed me when they were playing in the next room. I often yelled, "Keep your voices down! I can't stand all this noise!"

My unemployment insurance ran out in November. I felt hopeless. I couldn't support my family. And Christmas was coming. My family had always enjoyed Christmas. But this year, I was worried. I didn't want to disappoint my family. But with less money, how would I buy toys for the boys?

One day, I was walking downtown with my little boy, Bobby. As we walked along the streets, Bobby pointed to the big, beautiful Christmas trees in the store windows. He pointed to the Christmas toys. At one store, Bobby stopped and pointed to an electric train. "That's what I want for Christmas, Daddy!" he said. "Can I have it?" I was so choked up that I couldn't answer. I just pulled him away from that window and kept walking.

I still had not told my children that I was unemployed. My boys had always looked up to me. I couldn't face them with the truth that I couldn't support them.

One morning, my wife sat down on the bed and took my face in her hands. I couldn't avoid her eyes. "Roy," she said, "the boys don't understand what's wrong. They think that you must be sick or that you don't love them any more. Don't be so proud, Roy. Tell the boys what's wrong. They'll still love you. I do."

That night after dinner, I joined my boys in the living room. I told them what had happened. "I'm still looking for a job," I said. "But it's not likely that I'll find one before Christmas. So we'll have less money to spend for gifts this year. You'll get fewer toys, and they won't cost very much. I'm sorry about that." My voice shook as I talked.

"Oh, Daddy," said my older son, Jimmy. "I'm glad to know what's wrong. I thought you were sick. You slept so much that I was afraid you were going to die. If we need money, I can help. The neighbors will pay me to clean the snow off their walks."

My younger son, Bobby, ran to his room and came back with his toy bank. He opened it up and shook out the coins. "Here, Daddy," he said. "You take the coins I've been saving." He hugged me as he put the coins in my hand.

I hugged the boys and thanked them. What great sons! That night I slept better than I had for months.

Just before Christmas, one of my friends told me about a job opening at the factory where he worked. They needed someone to oil and repair the machines. I was able to see the employment officer there the next day. I told him about the job I had had for almost 10 years. I said I was good at repairing, cleaning, and oiling machines.

The employment officer said I would have to join the union. The job paid less than my last job. And this factory was noisier and dirtier. But I was glad when the employment officer shook my hand and told me to start work the following Monday.

I'll always remember that awful year. Now that it's past, I can talk about it. It was the lowest point in my life. If my wife and boys had not been so understanding, our family might not be together today.

Story Checkup

during (duur' ing)

Answer each question with one or two sentences.

1. What are some facts that Roy tells about himself?

____

____

2. What were some of the feelings that Roy had during this year of unemployment?

____

____

3. What do you think Roy learned during his year of unemployment?

____

____

Practice

Add the ending *-less* to each root word. Write the new word in the blank.

Example: hope hopeless

1. home ______________
2. care ______________
3. sleep ______________
4. friend ______________

Fill in each blank with one of the new words with *-less*.
You may use the word in the example, also.

1. The family was left ______________ after the fire.
2. The fire started because someone was ______________ with matches.
3. After many months without a job, I felt ______________.
4. I spent many ______________ nights during that year.
5. When Luke first moved to a big city, he felt ______________.

apply (u plȳ')	experience (ex pēr' ē ens)
grade	signature (sig' nu chur)

To apply for most jobs, you must fill out a job application. Complete the job application below. Pick a job that you would like to apply for. Give your own school and work experience. Sign your own name on the signature line.

JOB APPLICATION

Please print.

Name	Telephone
Address	Social Security No.
	U.S. citizen ☐ Yes ☐ No
Job you are applying for	Date you can start

Work experience: Begin with your latest job.

Name & address of employer	Kind of business	From: MO/YR	To: MO/YR	Work you did	Rate of pay	Why you left
1.						
2.						
3.						

Service experience:

Were you in the U.S. armed services? ☐ Yes ☐ No	From: MO/YR	To: MO/YR
Branch of service	Work you did in armed services	

School and other training: Circle highest grade completed.

Grade School 1 2 3 4 5 6 7 8	High School 1 2 3 4	College 1 2 3 4

	Name of school	Address of school	From: MO/YR	To: MO/YR
Grade School				
High School				
College				
Other training				

Do you:

have a driver's license? ☐ Yes ☐ No	own an automobile? ☐ Yes ☐ No	want to work nights? ☐ Yes ☐ No
List machines you know how to run.		

Signature ______________________

Add the ending *-ment* to each root word. Write the new word in the blank.

Example: employ employment

1. pay ____________________
2. agree ____________________
3. amuse ____________________
4. state ____________________

Fill in each blank with one of the new words with *-ment.*
You may use the word in the example, also.

1. I make a ____________________ on my car loan every month.
2. My landlady and I came to an ____________________ about the rent.
3. The children enjoyed the rides at the ____________________ park.
4. The state ____________________ office sent me to many companies to look for a job.
5. The man made a false ____________________ about the money he has.

In each line, circle the word that has the same meaning as the first word.

Example:

shout	talk	(yell)	speak
1. repair	broke	fix	sell
2. finish	fast	start	end
3. unhappy	happy	sad	sick
4. almost	nearly	all	quickly
5. quick	slow	quiet	fast
6. start	stop	begin	end
7. allow	show	alone	permit
8. small	huge	large	little

More Reading with *ū, oo, uu, ou, aw,* and *oy*

music ū	cure u-e	argue ue	few ew	
food oo	June u-e	blue ue	chew ew	
student ū or oo	Duke u-e	Tuesday ue	news ew	
book uu				
mouth ou	town ow			
lawn aw	Paul au	ball all	caught aught	bought ought
boy oy	oil oi			

Finding What You Want in Your Newspaper

health (helth)	advertise (ad' ver tize)	according (u cord' ing)
movie (moo' vē)	classified (clas' i fīd)	belong (bē long')
section (sec' shun)	different (dif' runt)	bottom (bot' um)
through (throo)	editor (ed' i ter)	sharp
	editorial (ed i tor' ē ul)	thankful (thank' ful)

- What's happening in my city?
- What's on TV tonight?
- Are there any job openings I could apply for?

You can find the answers to these questions, and many others, in different parts of your newspaper.

News stories give the facts about things that have happened in your city, the country, and the world. The main news stories start on the front page of the first section.

One part of the newspaper is marked so that you can tell it is not news. This part is called the editorial page. In editorials, editors try to get readers to agree with their ideas. The editorial page also has letters from readers. Through letters to the editor, we can all have a voice in the newspaper.

The family life section has stories about food, clothes, health, and ways to get the most for your money. This section may be called by different names in different newspapers.

Another section tells about TV shows, movies, and other things to see or do for fun.

People who get a newspaper mainly for sports turn to the sports section first. The sports section is found near the back of most newspapers.

Ads are found in all sections of the newspaper. Through advertising, companies can tell readers what they have to sell. And, through advertising, readers can find out about things they want to buy.

One section of the paper has only ads. That is the classified ad section. Both businesses and readers can advertise in this section. In the classified ads, small ads are grouped together under headings like Help Wanted or Autos for Sale.

This lesson has examples from different parts of the newspaper. This lesson will give you an idea of what you can find in your own newspaper.

NEWS STORY

Oil truck turns over, fire destroys two homes

Two houses near downtown were destroyed by fire this morning. The fire was caused by an 18-wheel truck hauling 10,000 gallons of oil.

John Howard of New York City was the driver of the truck. According to police, Howard was driving down Lewis Hill along Hill St. about 5 a.m. He could not make a sharp turn at the bottom of the hill, and the truck turned over. Howard was able to crawl from his truck and was not hurt.

Oil from the truck caught fire as it ran down the street. Two houses at the corner of Hill St. and Maple Ave. caught fire. By the time fire trucks arrived, the houses were almost destroyed.

The house at 101 Maple Ave., which belonged to Center City Land Company, was empty. The house at 100 Hill St. belonged to Mr. and Mrs. Paul Robinson. They were out of town.

Mary Garcia, of 105 Maple Ave., told reporters what she saw. According to Garcia, she was out walking her dog at the time of the accident.

"The truck couldn't make the sharp turn at the bottom of the hill," Garcia said. "The next thing I knew, the truck was over on its side. I saw the truck driver crawl out and run. Then I heard a big noise, and the oil caught fire. The burning oil was like a river of fire as it ran down to the houses."

Garcia ended by saying, "I'm glad no one was hurt. I'm sorry that the Robinsons' home was destroyed. But I'm thankful that the burning oil didn't get as far as my house."

mess	aide (aid)	grand	Mon. (Monday)
sidewalk (side' walk)	hour (our)	male	Fri. (Friday)
mental (men' tul)	lost	female (fē' male)	Aug. (August)
depress (dē press')	wash (wosh)	self	Sept. (September)

LETTERS TO THE EDITOR

Dogs have rights, too

Dear Editor:

In Tuesday's paper, J.D. said that his neighbor's dog messed up his lawn. The lawns should be fenced in, not the dogs.

Pets have rights, too. And one of them is the right to run. It's not fair to keep a healthy dog tied up all the time. There ought to be a law against it.

—Carlos Smith

Those dirty dogs!

Dear Editor:

I agree with J.D. that the city should crack down on owners who let their dogs run free. Not only do they dig up the lawns, but they also mess up the sidewalks. There ought to be a law to make the dog owners clean up after their dogs. I'm tired of the mess dogs make.

—G.P.

EDITORIAL

Get truck traffic off Lewis Hill

It's time for our town to do something to stop accidents at the bottom of Lewis Hill.

The awful accident this morning at the corner of Hill St. and Maple Ave. should get our council moving.

This is the sixth accident there in two years. Four of them were caused by big trucks that couldn't make the sharp turn on Hill St.

We can all be thankful that no one has been killed in these accidents. But unless we do something soon, someone will be killed.

For a long time, this newspaper has been saying that we need a new highway around our town. Then we could keep big trucks off Hill St.

We need state help to build that highway. Please call or write your council person. Tell him or her to ask the state for help NOW, before it's too late.

FAMILY LIFE

Being out of work can make you sick

Unemployment and health problems go together. This was the finding of a new study by the Center for Work and Mental Health in Washington, D.C.

Doctors across the country took part in the study. Information from them showed more sickness in places where many people are out of work. The study found that unemployed people smoke and drink more. They hit their children more. And they have more family fights.

"People show they are under stress in different ways," says the study report. "Some get sick. Others become angry or depressed. They drink too much or become violent."

Two out of every four laid-off workers at one factory reported that they could not sleep. Others said they could not eat or got sick when they did. These are signs of mental stress.

According to the study, most people can stand a few weeks of unemployment without health problems. The hardest time comes when unemployment insurance stops. After a year, unemployed workers often feel so hopeless that they stop looking for a job.

If you are unemployed, what can you do to avoid health problems? Doctors at the Center for Work and Mental Health give these answers.

You are almost sure to feel angry and depressed.

(continued on page 107)

Unemployment and your health

(continued from page 106)

But you should not keep these feelings to yourself. Bring them out in the open.

Don't be angry with yourself. It's not your fault that business is bad. Many people are out of work. You are just one of many hurt by hard times.

Talk openly with your family about your feelings. Talk about the problems all of you will face. In this way, your family can feel that you are all helping each other in a time of trouble. And you will not feel alone.

Tell children the truth. They will know that something is wrong anyway.

Try to make the most of your free time. Do some jobs at home that you have been putting off. Learn how to do something you have always wanted to learn. Spend time with your family and friends even if you don't have much money to spend.

Don't avoid telling people that you are out of work. The more people who know, the better chance you have to hear about job openings.

Above all, don't give up looking for a job. Going from place to place and hearing "no" is depressing. But if you stop looking, you have little chance of finding a job.

Classifieds

HELP WANTED

Auto repairs—Work on used cars, 3-5 years experience needed. Apply in person to City Auto Sales, 350 Dawson St. 2-5 p.m. Mon.-Fri.

Baker—24 hours a week. Experienced, all kinds of bread. The Bread Basket, 789 Fourth Ave., 7-9 p.m., Mon.-Fri.

Car wash—Full time. No experience needed. Fast worker, over 18 years old. Apply Cal's Car Wash, 218 Main.

Cook—Experienced and fast. Apply Terry's, 645 Maple St., 9-11 a.m.

Home health aide—Take care of sick people in their homes. Some cooking, cleaning, and child care. Apply to Lewis County Department of Health, 244 Main St., Mrs. Wong.

Kitchen helper—Oak Park Country Club, 2-4 p.m., Mon.-Fri.

Laundry—Person to run self-service coin laundry 8-12 nights. Lee's Wash & Dry, Grand Shopping Center.

Nurse's aide—Will train. Good pay & hours. Friendly person to work with older people. Shaw's Nursing Home, 351 Park Road. 479-7999.

Teacher's aide—Part time, mornings. Experience with small children. Oak Park School, 476-2131.

Truck driver—48-state carrier. Good driving record. Over 25 and belong to union. 451-2364.

LOST AND FOUND

Cat—Male, black, white on back and neck. Lost near Oak Park High School Aug. 29. Call 571-8907.

Cat—Female, gray. Found Sept. 1 near First Ave. and Lewis St. Call 572-9870 after 5.

Dog—Male, black and brown. White feet. Short hair. Lost Aug. 31 at Grand Shopping Center. 571-6344.

Glasses—Found Porter's Department Store, Aug. 30. Call in person.

Puppy—Female, 10 months old. Light brown with white face. Lost Sept. 2 near Front St. 663-4053.

Ring—Gold wedding band found Sept. 1 in ladies' room Newman's. 481-9805.

PETS FOR SALE

Birds—Many kinds, some talkers. Bright colors. Easy to care for. Bird World. 6519 Main St.

Cat—Free to good home. 2-year-old female. All shots. 542-8765.

Dog—Short-haired pointer. Male, trained, 2 years old. Moving out of state. 447-9087 after 5.

Tonight on TV

	6:00	6:30	7:00	7:30	8:00	8:30	9:00	9:30
3	News	NBC News	Around Town	Roy Hall	Movie of the Week: "It Came Out of the Fog"			
5	News	CBS News	Wild Country	Law & You	Voices of Thanksgiving		Mothers & Daughters	
9	News	ABC News	True or False	Open Phone	Football: New York at Washington			
10	News							
24	Health	Business	At the Movies	Meet Your City Council		The New China		Small Talk

Story Checkup

offer (off' er)

Write a short answer to each question.

1. What is the headline for the news story? ______________________________

____

2. What are three important facts that are given in the news story?

____

____

____

3. In the editorial, what idea does the newspaper offer for stopping accidents on Hill Street?

____

4. In the letters to the editor, which letter writer do you agree with? Why? ______________

____

5. Who did the study on unemployment and health problems? ______________________

____

6. In the Help Wanted ads, which job offers training? ______________________

7. What is the TV Movie of the Week? ______________________________

What time does it start? ______________________________

Practice

In each line, circle the words that have the same vowel sound as the first word.

1. law	low	haul	taught	laid
2. oil	coin	cool	Joyce	cook
3. ought	out	voice	moon	caught
4. boy	buy	join	book	toy
5. cloud	town	claw	call	plow
6. fault	fall	Paul	few	false

In each line, circle the word that means the opposite of the first word.

1. lost	last	found	saw	kept
2. bottom	side	last	rear	top
3. female	woman	manager	male	human
4. employed	destroyed	unemployed	disappointed	working
5. right	bad	good	wrong	write
6. true	fair	false	fault	right
7. same	alike	almost	different	nearly
8. large	most	major	complete	small
9. quiet	noisy	truth	depressed	sharp
10. less	mess	more	often	all
11. healthy	well	worry	hopeless	sick
12. always	never	also	almost	might

Write the missing ending in each blank.

-ful -less -ly -ment -ness -y

1. To stay health__________, you should eat right and get enough sleep.
2. Roy read the employ__________ ads in the newspaper every day.
3. The news reporter thought that Mary Garcia's story sounded truth__________.
4. We can all be thank__________ that no one was hurt in the accident.
5. The word *ad* is a short form for the word *advertise*__________.
6. I'm sorry that my thought__________ words hurt your feelings.
7. Everyone remembers Mrs. Brunoski's good__________ to those in trouble.
8. The new employee did the work quickly, but he was often care__________.
9. Being unemployed can cause sick__________.
10. At first, Roy kept his disappoint__________ to himself.
11. The house was complete__________ destroyed by fire.
12. She washed her dirt__________ hands.

consonant (con' su nunt)

Four Sounds for *s*

s* = *s* as in *snake	***s* = *z* as in *eggs***
***s* = *s* at the beginning of most words** see said step smile swim	
***s* = *s* at the end of these words** *gas yes this bus us	***s* = *z* at the end of these words** has his was as is
s* = *s* when a word ends with a consonant and *se false nurse license	
s* = *s* in some words that end with a vowel and *se base house	***s* = *z* in some words that end with a vowel and *se*** raise these rose noise amuse
s* = *s* when *s* comes before the sound for the consonants *p, t, k *aspirin yesterday basket rescue	***s* = *z* when *s* comes before other consonants or vowel sounds** husband easy visit thousand Tuesday cousin music president
s* = *s* when the *-s* ending follows the sound for the consonants *p, t, k, f lips hats looks *cuffs helps hunts picks laughs hopes gates likes picnics	***s* = *z* when the *-s* or *-es* ending follows other consonants or vowel sounds** jobs plays ties faces beds trees cries pages dogs chews babies boxes loves laws goes dishes calls radios tomatoes watches
***ss* = *s* in most words** miss discuss lesson possible	

s* = *sh* as in *sure	***s* = *zh* as in *measure***
***s* = *sh* in these words** sure insurance *issue (ish' oo) sugar *pressure (presh' ur)	***s* = *zh* in these words** *measure (mezh' ur) *usual (ū' zhoo ul) *pleasure (plezh' ur) *usually

*New words

1. The Moon Shines On

doesn't	seem	Kansas (Kan' zus)	unpleasant
moon	shine	remark (rē mark')	passenger (pas' en jer)
rode	excuse (ex cuze')	pleasant (plez' unt)	

In Kansas City, I met a man I will never forget. He was a bus driver in Kansas City. He usually drove at night, and I often rode home from work with him.

I used to watch him as the passengers got on the bus. He had a pleasant smile for each one. It was a pleasure to see how many passengers lost their frowns and smiled back.

There was one passenger who never smiled back. He usually pushed his way onto the bus and hurried to sit down. When he climbed over other passengers, he never excused himself. When he stepped on their feet, he never excused himself. He was rude, but that didn't stop the bus driver's smile. The driver gave the unpleasant man his usual bright smile.

The rude man never seemed to see that smile. He would blow his nose loudly and make unpleasant remarks about the way the bus driver was driving. He usually made one or two unpleasant remarks each night, and he made sure everyone heard them.

The rude man's remarks took the pleasure out of the ride for me. But the bus driver never seemed upset. He just went on smiling at the passengers as they got on and off the bus.

I wanted to get to know this friendly bus driver, so one night I rode the bus to the end of the line.

"Excuse me," I said. "I have wanted to tell you what a pleasure it is to have a driver like you. You're the friendliest bus driver in Kansas City. But why don't you throw that one rude man off the bus?"

The bus driver gave me one of his brightest smiles. "That man doesn't annoy me," he said. "Let me tell you about my neighbor's dog. The man next door to me has a dog. Every time the moon shines, the dog barks and barks."

"Well," I asked, "what about the dog and the moon?"

"Oh," he said, "the moon keeps on shining."

Three Sounds for *ch*

ch = *ch* as in *child*

***ch* = *ch* in most words**

child	* chip		each	lunch	catch	rich
choke	* choose	(chooz)	peach	branch	match	which
chair	* chose	(choze)	teach	march	watch	much
check	* Charles	(Charlz)	* speech	church	stitch	* such
chart	* chocolate	(choc' u lut)			kitchen	touch
					* Mitchell	sandwich

ch = *k* as in *Christmas*

***ch* = *k* in some words**

Christmas	school		* chorus	(kor' us)	* Michael	(Mi' kul)
* Chris	* schedule	(skej' ule)	* chemistry	(kem' is try)	* mechanic	(me kan' ic)

ch = *sh* as in *machine*

***ch* = *sh* in a few words**

machine	* Chicago	(Shi cog' ō)	* chef	(shef)
	* Charlotte	(Shar' lot)	* Chevy	(Shev' y)

*New words

2. Open House at Central High School

I'd	homeroom	central (sen' trul)	notice (nō' tis)
here's	lunchroom	cookie (cook' y)	program (prō' gram)
wouldn't	welcome	gym (jim)	

"Look, Mother! Here's a notice about the open house at my school." Chris handed her mother the notice.

> ***Welcome to Open House***
>
> *Chicago Central High School*
> *Wednesday, October 18*
> *7:30 p.m.*
>
> *(Please bring a cake or cookies.)*

Charlotte Mitchell read the notice and thanked her daughter. "I wouldn't miss it," she said. "Your dad and I always welcome the chance to meet your teachers."

"Can you bake some chocolate chip cookies?" Chris wanted to know.

"You and your brother Michael can bake them," her mother answered.

Chris and her younger brother baked the cookies. Charlotte made sure that her husband Charles was free on Wednesday evening.

At dinner on Wednesday, Chris told her parents she wouldn't ride to school with them because she had chorus practice at 6:30. She would meet them at her homeroom.

By 7:30, Mr. and Mrs. Mitchell and Michael arrived at the school in their old Chevy. They took the cookies to the lunchroom and went to meet Chris.

Chris's homeroom teacher met them at the door and said, "Welcome to Chicago Central High. Here's your daughter's schedule of classes. You may choose the classes you wish to visit. The bell will ring when the program is ready to begin in the gym."

Charles Mitchell looked at the schedule and said, "I'll choose social studies, chemistry, and English."

His wife looked at the schedule and said, "I'll choose the machine shop and math." Then, both of them chose to go to the cooking class.

Chris chose to go along with her father. Michael chose to join his mother because he wanted to see the machine shop.

The chemistry teacher told Chris's father that she was a good student. Chris said, "Some girls don't like chemistry, but I do. We wouldn't have many of the good things in life without chemistry."

The Mitchells all met at the cooking class. Mr. Mitchell wanted to know if there were any male students. "Oh, sure," the teacher said. "Almost everyone will live alone at some time in his life. So everyone should know how to cook. And some of my students will become chefs. Being a chef is a good job for both men and women."

"When I get to high school, I'd like to study auto mechanics," Michael told his parents. "Then, when you give your old Chevy to Chris and me, I can be the mechanic. I'll be the best mechanic in Chicago, and I'll keep that old Chevy running forever!"

Just then, the Mitchells heard the bell ring for the start of the program in the gym. Chris ran to take her place in the chorus. Everyone enjoyed the chorus and the speeches. They were glad that the speeches were short.

After the program in the gym, all the parents and their children went into the lunchroom. The Mitchells saw their chocolate chip cookies on the big table with lots of other cookies and cakes.

As they rode home that night, the Mitchells talked about the open house. "We had such a good time," Mrs. Mitchell said. "I enjoyed your teachers, the classes, the chorus, and even the speeches."

Story 1: The Moon Shines On

Answer each question in a few words.

1. In what city did the story take place? ________________________

2. How did the bus driver try to make his passengers happy? ________________________

____

3. What showed that one passenger was rude? ________________________

____

4. What did the bus driver do when the rude man made unpleasant remarks? ________________________

____

5. Do you think the title of the story is a good one? Why or why not? ________________________

____

Story 2: Open House at Central High School

In what order did these things happen?
Put a number by each sentence to show the right order.

_____ Chris's homeroom teacher welcomed Mr. and Mrs. Mitchell.

_____ Chris and Michael baked chocolate chip cookies for the open house.

_____ The open house ended with snacks in the school lunchroom.

_____ Chris went to chorus practice at 6:30 on Wednesday.

_____ The Mitchells went to the gym for the program.

_____ Chris's parents visited some of her classes.

_____ Mr. and Mrs. Mitchell arrived at the school in their old Chevy.

_____ Chris brought home a notice about an open house at her high school.

flour	beaten	salt (sawlt)	vanilla (vu nil' u)
mix	spoon	soda (sō' du)	¼ (one fourth)
nut	teaspoon	measure (mezh' ur)	½ (one half)
stir	sift	recipe (res' i pē)	⅔ (two thirds)
beat	soft	shortening (short' ning)	¾ (three fourths)

Read this recipe, and write short answers to the questions below.

Chocolate Chip Cookies

Mix by hand with a large spoon, or use electric mixer.
Use a measuring cup and measuring spoons.

1. Mix well 2/3 cup soft shortening (part butter), 3/4 cup white sugar , 1/2 cup brown sugar (packed)
2. Add, and stir in 2 well-beaten eggs, 1 1/2 teaspoons vanilla
3. Sift together 2 cups sifted flour 1 teaspoon salt and stir in1 teaspoon baking soda
4. Stir in1 large bag of chocolate chips, 1/4 cup broken nuts
5. Drop from teaspoon onto cookie pan. Leave space between cookies.
6. Bake 8 to 10 minutes at 375°. Cookies should still be soft. Cool for a few minutes before removing from pan.

Makes about 50 cookies.

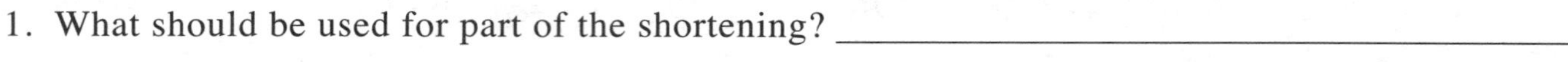

1. What should be used for part of the shortening? ______
2. What do you do to the brown sugar as you measure it? ______
3. In the first step of this recipe, what things do you mix together? ______

______

4. In the second step of this recipe, what things do you add and stir in? ______

______

5. Do you beat the eggs before you add them to the shortening and sugar? ______
6. Are the flour, salt, and baking soda added before or after the eggs? ______
7. Do you sift the sugar with the flour, salt, and baking soda? ______
8. How much vanilla is used in this recipe? ______
9. What is stirred in at the same time as the nuts? ______
10. How long should you bake the cookies? ______

Practice

In each line, circle the words in which *s* has the same sound as in the first word.

Example:	is	bus	(has)	(rose)	gas
1.	seem	yes	step	cousin	miss
2.	pleasant	music	base	noise	these
3.	pleasure	discuss	usual	stops	measure
4.	passenger	class	easy	boxes	this

In each line, circle the words in which *ch* has the same sound as in the first word.

1.	child	chip	chorus	chef	choose
2.	Christmas	machine	mechanic	school	Charles
3.	Chicago	chose	speech	Chevy	machine
4.	lunch	watch	Michael	chocolate	Charlotte

Homework

Read the two words, and then write the contraction for them.

1. I have ____________________
2. here is ____________________
3. could not ____________________
4. does not ____________________
5. they will ____________________
6. would not ____________________

Put together a word from List 1 with a word from List 2 to make a compound word.

	List 1	List 2	Compound Word
1.	class	town	____________________
2.	grand	spoon	____________________
3.	down	room	____________________
4.	side	children	____________________
5.	tea	walk	____________________

Two Sounds for *c*

c = *k* as in *cup*	*c* = *s* as in *city*
_c_ = _k_ before a consonant class cry * scream act back	
_c_ = _k_ before _a, o,_ or _u_ **_ca_ _co_ _cu_** cat cop cut	**_c_ = _s_ before _e, i,_ or _y_** **_ce_ _ci_ _cy_** cent city icy
_cc_ = _k_ before _a, o,_ or _u_ **_cca_ _cco_ _ccu_** * occasion (o kā' zhun) according * occupation (ok ū pā' shun)	**_cc_ = _ks_ before _e_ or _i_** **_cce_ _cci_** * accept (ak sept') accident
_c_ = _k_ at the end of a word music public * medic	**_ce_ = _s_ at the end of a word** face service * difference

Two Sounds for *g*

g = *g* as in *go*	*g* = *j* as in *age*
_g_ = _g_ before a consonant glass glad grow grade *Grace	
_g_ = _g_ before _a, o,_ or _u_ **_ga_ _go_ _gu_** game got gun	**_g_ = _j_ before _e, i,_ or _y_** **_ge_ _gi_ _gy_** * gentle (jen' tul) * Ginger (Jin' jer) * energy (en' er jy) Note: In a few words, _g_ = _g_ before _e_ or _i_. Some examples are _get, gift, girl, give_.
_gg_ = _g_ even before _e, i,_ or _y_ bigger hugging foggy	
_g_ = _g_ at the end of a word leg big hug fog dig rug dog	**_ge_ or _dge_ = _j_ at the end of a word** age courage change * edge page * bandage * strange * bridge

* New words

A Strange Tale of War

aid	graduate (graj' oo ate)
army	lay
Chang	shoot
danger (dān' jer)	soldier (sōl' jer)
enemy	tale
Gene	themselves
Gordon	wound (woond)

It was strange how much alike Gene Bridges and Gordon Chang were. When they were young, they both took care of hurt animals. They bandaged the animals and nursed them back to health. They enjoyed helping the animals get well.

Gene Bridges and Gordon Chang both longed to become doctors so they could help people get well. They both learned to give first aid. They read many books about doctors with great courage. In the books they read, doctors gave their lives and their energy to helping people in sickness and danger. Both Gene and Gordon longed to be doctors like that.

How much alike Gene and Gordon were! There seemed to be only one difference between them. They lived in different countries on opposite sides of the world.

When Gene graduated from high school, it was a proud occasion for the Bridges family. Gene was accepted by a college near his home. He hoped to work his way through college and become a doctor. Gordon Chang graduated from high school the same year Gene did. It was a proud occasion for the Chang family, too. Gordon was also accepted by a college and hoped to become a doctor.

But just after Gene and Gordon graduated from high school, their countries called them to war. Before he went off to war, Gene married his girlfriend Ginger. Gordon married Grace, the girl he loved.

In the armed services, both Gene and Gordon became medics. Each was a medic in his own country's army. (Medics rescue soldiers who have been wounded in the fighting. They give first aid and other emergency care.)

All their lives, both Gene and Gordon had wanted to help other people. They were gentle men. It was hard for them to accept war and killing. Many times, their hearts grew heavy, and they felt very tired. But they found new energy to rescue and bandage wounded soldiers. They tried to forget the hurt in their gentle hearts.

The medics went where the fighting was going on. They carried out wounded soldiers. On those occasions, the medics carried guns to protect themselves. Gene and Gordon didn't like carrying guns, but they knew there was danger. They could get shot. Each of them hoped that he would never have to shoot another man.

Gene wrote to his wife Ginger. He said he didn't like being in this strange country. He wanted to be with Ginger and their baby girl who had been born while he was away.

Gordon didn't like war any more than Gene did. He read the letters from his wife Grace over and over. He, too, longed to go home and see their new baby boy.

It's true that Gene and Gordon were very much alike. But now there was a big difference between them. Because their countries were at war, they were enemies.

One long hot day, bombs were falling, and there was a lot of shooting. Gene was sick of bandaging arms and legs that were half shot off. He was sick of seeing young men with parts of their faces missing. By the time the sun began to go down, Gene had no energy left. Then he heard a scream from the edge of the river. Gene knew he would be walking into danger if he went there. It was an open place. But he heard the scream again. His heart jumped. He would have to go to the edge of the river to get that wounded soldier.

As he ran to the screaming soldier, Gene heard a sound from across the river. He looked up and saw an enemy standing over a wounded man. The enemy saw him at the same time.

Both of them went for their guns. It was shoot or be shot. They both shot.

Two medics lay dying on the edges of the river. Gene Bridges would never know that the man he shot was Gordon Chang. He would never know that the last thing he did in life was to kill a man who was as gentle and kind as he. Gordon Chang would never know the kind of man he killed.

So ends the strange tale of two gentle-hearted men.

Story Checkup

Write sentence answers.

1. What were four ways in which Gene Bridges and Gordon Chang were alike?

____

____

____

____

2. What was one way in which the two men were different? ______________________________

____

3. Why were the two men enemies? ______________________________

____

4. What do you think is the main idea of this story? ______________________________

____

Practice

In each line, circle the words that *begin* with the same sound as the first word.

1. cup	cat	cent	city	class	cry
2. city	civil	cause	center	citizen	cabin
3. game	good	Ginger	Grace	gentle	Gail
4. jump	gold	Gene	gym	gun	Ginger

In each line, circle the words that *end* with the same sound as the first word.

1. miss	music	house	price	back	service
2. bake	back	medic	space	ice	picnic
3. leg	page	fog	bridge	egg	big
4. age	edge	hug	huge	strange	large

enroll (en rōll')	register (rej' is ter)	citizenship (cit' izen ship)
mail	registration (rej is trā' shun)	political (pu lit' i cul)
middle	occupation (oc ū pā' shun)	Democratic (Dem u crat' ic)
present (prez' unt)	election (ē lec' shun)	Republican (Rē pub' lic un)
	residence (rez' i dence)	

If you want to vote in elections, you must register to vote. Voter registration forms can be different from state to state. But most registration forms ask for the same kinds of information.

Fill out this voter registration form for yourself. In the blank marked *Occupation,* print *Student* if you go to school full time.

VOTER REGISTRATION FORM—PLEASE PRINT

Last name	First name	Middle or maiden name

RESIDENCE ADDRESS: House no. and street name	Apt. no.	City	State	Zip code

MAILING ADDRESS (If different from residence address): Post office box or route	City	State	Zip code

Telephone no.	Date of birth: MM/DD/YYYY	Sex ☐Male ☐Female	Race or ethnic group ☐American Indian or Alaskan Native ☐Black/not Hispanic ☐Hispanic ☐Asian or Pacific Islander ☐White/not Hispanic ☐Multi-racial ☐Other
			Choice of party ☐Democratic Party ☐Green Party ☐Libertarian Party ☐Republican Party ☐Other ____________ ☐I do not wish to enroll in any political party

State ID or driver's license no.	Social Security No. (if you do not have a state driver's license or ID no.)

Occupation	Name & address of employer or school

Have you ever voted in an election before in this state? ☐**Yes** ☐**No** **If yes, complete the following line.**

In what year did you last vote in an election in this state?	Did you register under your present name? ☐Yes ☐No	If not, under what name did you register?	Did you then live at your present address? ☐Yes ☐No If no, give address then. Street ____________ City ____________

Are you a citizen of the United States of America? ☐**Yes** ☐**No** | **Will you be at least 18 years of age on or before election day?** ☐**Yes** ☐**No**

If you checked "No" to either of these questions, do not fill out this form.

I state that the information I have given here is true.

____
Date Signature

FOR OFFICE USE ONLY Voter registration no. ____________

____
Last name First name Middle name

____
Street address

Write *True* if the sentence is true. Write *False* if the sentence is false.

__________ 1. Gene Bridges and Gordon Chang were from the same country.

__________ 2. The Bridges family and the Chang family were good friends.

__________ 3. Gene and Gordon became doctors before they went off to war.

__________ 4. Gene and Gordon both became medics in the armed services.

__________ 5. The war took place in Gene's country.

__________ 6. Gordon's wife was named Grace.

__________ 7. Gene went to the edge of the river to rescue a wounded soldier.

__________ 8. The story tells which country won the war.

Write the missing ending in each blank.

-al   -hood   -ment   -ship

1. I don't need citizen__________ papers because I was born in this country.
2. The Fourth of July is a nation__________ holiday in the United States.
3. Martin Luther King's leader__________ helped blacks get more civil rights.
4. Tran Ty Lan often thought of her child__________ in Vietnam.
5. The enroll__________ in our English class is bigger than last year.
6. Chris will sing in a music__________ program at the high school tonight.
7. Baseball is a season__________ sport.
8. The neighbor__________ changed from a rich one to a poor one.
9. Lan was thankful for Molly's friend__________.
10. Clocks give us a measure__________ of time.
11. Molly writes a lot of person__________ letters to friends and relatives.
12. In most states, the law says that adult__________ begins at the age of 18.

spell, silent (sī' lent)

Other Consonant Spellings

wr = r as in write

write wrote written	wrong	* wrap * wrinkle

kn = n as in know

know knew	* knee * kneel	* knob * knock

mb = m as in climb

climb bomb	* dumb * thumb	* crumb * limb

ph = f as in phone

phone telephone	nephew * elephant (el' u funt)	* physical (fiz' i cal) * physician (fiz i' shun)

gh = f as in laugh

laugh	* cough (cawf)	* rough (ruf) * tough (tuf) enough

Note: In some words, *gh* is silent. Some examples are:

through (throo)	* although (awl thō')	* weigh (wā)

*New words

1. Elephants Are Unusual Animals

pound	trunk	ivory (ī' ver y)	Africa (Af' ric u)
skin	tusk	Asia (ā' zhu)	African (Af' ric un)
smooth	bull (buul)	Asian (ā' zhun)	peaceful
thick	grown (grōwn)		unusual

The elephant is a very unusual animal. It is the largest animal that lives on land. No other animal has a nose that it uses as a hand. No other animal has ears that are four feet across and teeth that are six feet long.

Elephants may be called dumb animals. (We often call animals dumb because they cannot talk.) But elephants are not stupid. They can be trained to do many things. Some are trained to work in shows. They learn to kneel on their knees, stand on their heads, and even play baseball.

In Asia, elephants are often used as work animals. They can carry heavy loads. They can work on rough ground and in thick woods where machines cannot be used.

By wrapping its trunk around a tree, an elephant can pull up the tree by its roots. By running into a tree with its head, an elephant can knock down a tree. In this way, an elephant can knock down a tree that is 30 feet high.

The elephant's trunk may be its most unusual part. Its trunk may be six feet long and weigh 300 pounds. The elephant smells and gets food and water with its trunk. It can pick up something as small as a bread crumb or as large as the limb of a tree.

The elephant also feels with its trunk. The knobs at the end of its trunk act as fingers and thumbs. With these knobs, elephants can feel if something is rough or smooth, soft or hard.

The elephant's thick skin is very rough and wrinkled. Two of the elephant's teeth are very long. They are the tusks. The tusks are made of ivory. These ivory tusks are strong and smooth. They can be sold for a lot of money.

There are two kinds of elephants, those that live in Africa and those that live in Asia. Elephants in Africa are larger and harder to train than those in Asia. An African bull elephant may weigh 14,000 pounds. An African elephant has two knobs at the end of its trunk.

An Asian elephant has a shorter trunk with only one knob at the end. An Asian bull elephant may weigh 12,000 pounds. A cow elephant weighs from 5,000 to 10,000 pounds.

Elephants are full grown at 20 years of age. They live about 60 years. They are peaceful animals and have almost no enemies. Because full-grown elephants are large and tough, other animals don't try to hurt them. Only man, who kills elephants for their ivory, is their enemy.

Countries in both Asia and Africa have made laws to protect these unusual animals. Although there are such laws, elephants are still being killed.

2. Having a Physical Exam

adult	chest	exam	medicine (med' i cin)
appointment	clinic	important	pain
blood (blud)	deep	lab	pressure (presh' ur)
body			

Having a complete physical exam is a way of checking on the health of your body.

How often should an adult have a complete exam by a physician? The answer is different for different people.

You should have a physical exam *every year* if:

- you take medicine for long times.
- you have a long-lasting health problem.
- you are over 65 years of age.

You should have a physical exam *every two years* if you are between 40 and 65.

You should have a physical exam *every two–five years* if you are an adult under 40.

If you are changing doctors, it is important to have a complete physical exam.

If you don't have a doctor, you can find the names of doctors in the telephone directory. Look under *Physicians* in the yellow pages.

Some cities have free or low-cost public clinics. To find out about clinics where you live, phone your city or county health department.

You will need to make an appointment for your exam at a physician's office or at a clinic. You can make the appointment by telephone. When you phone, ask if there is anything you should bring. Ask about the cost of the exam and any lab tests you will need to have.

If you have health insurance, phone your insurance company. Ask what your insurance will pay for. Although insurance doesn't usually pay for physical exams, some lab tests may be covered.

When you arrive for your appointment, a nurse will talk to you first. She will ask about any sickness you have had and any medicine you are taking. She will weigh you and measure you.

The nurse or doctor will test your blood pressure. This test is very important. About one in ten Americans has high blood pressure. High blood pressure can cause very bad problems, but a person can have it and not know it.

The doctor will ask about any health problems you are having, such as pains or coughing. It is important to tell the doctor everything about how you feel. The doctor will look into your eyes, ears, nose, mouth, and throat.

The doctor will listen to your heart and chest. He or she will ask you to breathe deeply and then to cough. As you breathe deeply and cough, the doctor will listen to sounds in your heart and chest.

The doctor will check other parts of your body. He or she will take some blood for a blood test. The doctor may want you to have other lab tests.

If you have any questions during the exam, ask the doctor. Your physician should take the time to discuss things with you.

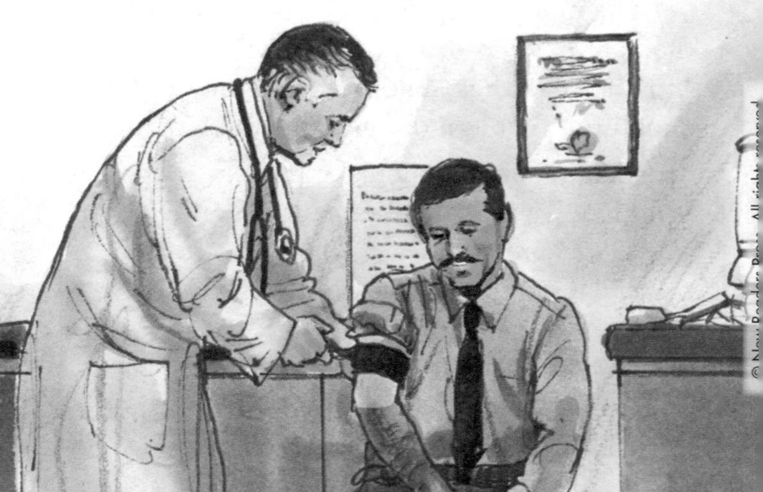

Write short answers to these questions.

Story 1: Elephants Are Unusual Animals

1. What are the two kinds of elephants? ____________________
2. Which kind of elephant is larger? ____________________
3. Which kind of elephant is easier to train? ____________________
4. Which kind of elephant has two knobs at the end of its trunk? ____________________
5. Which part of the elephant is the most unusual? ____________________
6. What are the elephant's tusks made of? ____________________
7. Who is the only enemy of a full-grown elephant? ____________________
8. How much may an African bull elephant weigh? ____________________

Story 2: Having a Physical Exam

1. Why is it important to have a physical exam? ____________________

   ____

2. According to the information in this story, how often should you yourself have a physical exam?

   ____

3. How can you find out about free or low-cost clinics where you live?

   ____

   ____

4. What should you ask when you phone for an appointment for your exam?

   ____

   ____

5. What are some of the things the doctor will do as part of the exam?

   ____

   ____

6. What are two important things for you to do during the exam?

   ____

   ____

Reading Directions on Medicines

ache (ake)	redness	soap	warn (worn)
headache	tablet	spray	direct (di rect')
dose	unless	minor (mī' ner)	direction (di rec' shun)
overdose	bite	once (wuns)	prescription (prē scrip' shun)
aspirin	case	taken	non-prescription
insect	reach		

There are some medicines that you can buy only with a doctor's prescription. There are other medicines that you can buy without a doctor's prescription. Non-prescription medicines, like the ones below, are for minor health problems. It is important to read the directions with care before you use *any* medicine—prescription or non-prescription.

ASPIRIN

For head colds, minor headaches, and other minor aches and pains.

Dose: (Take with water.)
Adults: 1 or 2 tablets
Children over 12 years: 1 tablet

For children under 12 years of age: Use aspirin only as directed by physician.

For adults: May be taken every 4 hours, up to 6 times daily.

For children: May be taken every 4 hours, up to 3 times daily.

Warning: Keep aspirin and all other medicine out of reach of children. In case of overdose, phone physician at once.

Cough Medicine

DIRECTIONS

Dose for adults and children over 12: Take 2 teaspoons every 4 hours. Do not take more than 12 teaspoons in 24 hours.

Dose for children 6 to 12: Take 1 teaspoon every 4 hours. Do not take more than 6 teaspoons in 24 hours.

Dose for children 2 to 6: Take 1/2 teaspoon every 4 hours. Do not take more than 3 teaspoons in 24 hours.

Do not give to children under 2 unless directed by physician.

WARNING: Persons with high blood pressure or heart problems should not use this medicine unless directed by physician.

Do not use for more than 10 days unless directed by physician.

Keep out of the reach of children.

FIRST AID SPRAY

Protects skin wounds. Takes pain out of minor burns and insect bites.

For minor cuts: First, gently clean the cut with soap and water. Dry the skin around the cut and apply First Aid Spray on the cut. May be covered with a clean bandage.

For minor burns and insect bites: Spray lightly onto skin.

Warning: Do not use on major cuts, deep wounds, bad burns, or animal bites. If redness or pain continues, stop using and see a physician. Spray should not be used on a cut for more than 10 days.

Use only on skin. Do not spray into eyes or mouth. Do not use on long-lasting skin problems.

Do not use on children under 2.

Practice

Underline each word that has the sound for *f*.

high	laugh	through	half	enough
phone	nephew	thumb	flour	tough
cough	crumb	elephant	night	chef
weigh	physical	office	foot	although

Underline each word in which two letters together stand for one consonant sound.

write	limb	stir	knob	phone
shoot	kneel	scream	cough	proud
wrong	brook	chip	dumb	tusk
knee	wrap	slept	long	according
sorry	accept	lesson	bomb	bull

Homework

Complete the sentence with the right word.

(know, no)	1. I ____________________ the answer to the question.
(our, hour)	2. You can do the work in one ____________________.
(knew, new)	3. I bought a ____________________ book today.
(right, write)	4. Gene will ____________________ a letter to his wife.
(male, mail)	5. Please ____________________ the letter for me.
(their, there)	6. I have never been to ____________________ house.
(road, rode)	7. Yesterday, I ____________________ home on the bus.
(through, threw)	8. They are afraid to walk ____________________ the park at night.
(wood, would)	9. I ____________________ like to visit Africa.
(flower, flour)	10. This cookie recipe calls for two cups of ____________________.

Words Ending in *-tion, -ssion, -sion*

-tion = shun as in *direction*

section	(sec' shun)	* nation	(nā' shun)
election	(ē lec' shun)	* station	(stā' shun)
direction	(di rec' shun)	* addition	(a di' shun)
contraction	(con trac' shun)	* education	(ej u cā' shun)
prescription	(prē scrip' shun)	* recreation	(rec rē ā' shun)
application	(ap li cā' shun)	* constitution	(con sti tū' shun)
information	(in for mā' shun)	* transportation	(trans por tā' shun)
registration	(rej is trā' shun)	* pronunciation	(prō nun cē ā' shun)

-ssion = shun as in *discussion*

* discussion	(dis cu' shun)
* depression	(dē pre' shun)
* admission	(ad mi' shun)

-sion = zhun as in *television*

* television	(tel' e vi zhun)
* decision	(dē ci' zhun)
occasion	(o cā' zhun)

*New words

The Ted Howard Show

art	guest (gest)	pronounce (prō nounce')
budget (buj' et)	hello	reason (rea' zun)
D'Angelo (Dē An' je lō)	Italy (It' u ly)	subject
decide (dē cide')	issue (ish' oo)	they're
diploma (di plō' mu)	Joseph (Jō' zeph or Jō' seph)	we'd
government (guv' ern ment)		

(This talk show takes place at public television station KRXT. It is called the "Ted Howard Show." Ted's guests are Gail Newman, Joseph D'Angelo, and Helen Baker.)

Ted Howard: Hello, this is Ted Howard for KRXT, your public television station. Tonight, we have a very important issue to discuss and three guests you will enjoy meeting.

Last week, we discussed budget cuts in education that our state government is planning. Tonight, we'll continue our discussion of this issue. Our three guests will tell what the budget cuts would mean to them. They are students at the Freedom Adult Education Center.

Gail Newman is on my left. Hello, Gail. Tell us your reason for enrolling at the Freedom Center.

Gail Newman: I decided to get my high school diploma. I never finished high school. The factory where I work was beginning to use more machines and fewer employees. I didn't know what I would do if I lost my job. The kinds of jobs that are open these days take more and more education.

Ted: It was a good idea to look ahead, Gail. What does an adult have to do to get a high school diploma?

Gail: You have to pass exams in all the important high school subjects. The admissions office at the center helped me find out what subjects I needed to study. I've passed the exams in every subject but math and writing.

Ted: Thanks, Gail. You seem to be moving ahead with your plans. Now let's hear from Joseph D'Angelo. Hello, Joseph. What are you studying?

Joseph D'Angelo: I'm studying to become a citizen. I came here from Italy about four years ago. I could not speak much English. Friends from Italy told me about the Freedom Center. I went to the admissions office. At that time, I could not even pronounce my street address, so they put me in the beginning class. My pronunciation still isn't so good. But I have learned a lot in my English class.

Ted: Your pronunciation sounds fine to me, Joseph. Tell us, what are you studying in addition to English?

Joseph: In my citizenship class, I am studying about this nation and its government. We have just started studying the Constitution.

Ted: That must be a pretty tough subject!

Joseph: Yes, but I like learning about the Constitution. In this nation, the Constitution protects our freedom.

Ted: That was a good speech, Joseph.

Joseph: It was not just a speech. I love this nation. I hope to become a citizen and vote in my first election next year.

Ted: Good for you! We could use more good citizens like you. Now let's meet Helen Baker. Your reason for taking classes was very different, wasn't it, Mrs. Baker?

Helen Baker: Please call me Helen. That makes me feel younger. Yes, my reason *was* different. After my husband died two years ago, I became very depressed. For many months, I just stayed at home, feeling sorry for myself. Then a friend brought me to her art class to get me out of my depression. The art class and being with other people did help me overcome my depression. Then I decided to take other classes just for recreation.

Ted: Some people say that recreation is not education.

Helen: Well, they're wrong. Some recreation classes, such as swimming, keep your body healthy. Others, like discussion groups, keep your mind growing.

Ted: Well, each of you seems to be finding something different in adult education. And the center seems to mean a lot to you. But, as you know, the future of Freedom Center is in question.

The city board of education has a hard decision to make. Next year, the state plans big cuts in the education budget. With less state money to spend on education, the school board says it may have to close Freedom Center. If that decision is made, what would it mean to you, Gail?

Gail: Oh, that would be awful! I would never get my high school diploma.

Ted: There is an adult education program at Mason County College. Couldn't you go there to study?

Gail: No, it costs more, and it's too far away. Transportation would be a problem. I don't have a car, and the bus would take too much time.

Ted: Would transportation be a problem for you, Joseph?

Joseph: No, I have a car. And I will be ready to take my citizenship exam soon. But I worry about my friends from Italy. Some of them cannot speak any English. It's hard for them to use public transportation. The Freedom Center is near our neighborhood, so they can walk to class now.

Ted: What about you, Helen? Is there a reason why you need to continue classes?

Helen: Yes, there *is* a reason. Older people who keep on learning live longer and enjoy life more. And they're more fun to be with.

Ted: We'd like to hear more from you, Helen, but we're running out of time.

My guests tonight have been speaking for the 300 students at the Freedom Adult Education Center. In addition, there are thousands of others with the same needs. Our city has 25,000 adults who, like Gail Newman, do not have a high school diploma. Joseph D'Angelo told us about his need to learn English. Each year, between two and three hundred people who do not speak English come to live in our city. And Helen Baker is only one out of 10,000 people over 60 living here.

Next year, the services that Freedom Center has for these people may be lost. I thank my guests for sharing in the discussion of this issue. Now, for television station KRXT, good night.

Story Checkup

amusement

Circle the letter of the right answer.

1. What was the subject of the discussion on this talk show?
   a. how to get a better job by taking classes
   b. what cuts in the education budget would mean to some students at the Freedom Center
   c. how to become a citizen
2. Why did Gail Newman enroll at the Freedom Center?
   a. to learn how to run a computer
   b. to be on Ted Howard's talk show
   c. to get her high school diploma
3. Why is Joseph D'Angelo studying at the center?
   a. to become a citizen of the U.S.A.
   b. to study about Italy
   c. to learn how to drive a car
4. Why does Helen Baker want to continue her classes?
   a. to get a college diploma
   b. to get a better job
   c. to enjoy life more

Practice

Match each word in the first list with a word in the second list that means the same thing. Write the letter in the blank. The first one is filled in for you.

C	1. exam	A. doctor
_____	2. chef	B. yell
_____	3. tale	C. test
_____	4. strange	D. part
_____	5. section	E. country
_____	6. recreation	F. story
_____	7. nation	G. unusual
_____	8. physician	H. amusement
_____	9. scream	I. cook

skill	safety	bookkeeping	improvement (im proov' ment)
dance	history	sew (sō)	Dec. (December)
square	blueprint	type (tȳp)	I (one)
Spanish	ballroom	course (cors)	II (two)
process	shorthand	retirement	III (three)

FREEDOM ADULT EDUCATION CENTER
1000 South Main Street

Registration
Sept. 6–9

Fall Schedule of Evening Classes
Classes Begin Week of Sept. 12, End Week of Dec. 12

For More Information
Call 486-3500

COURSE TITLE	Days*	Time
Language Arts		
Reading Improvement	M/W	7:00–9:00
Writing Improvement	T/Th	7:00–9:00
English as a Second Language	M/W	7:00–9:30
Public Speaking	T	7:00–9:00
Sign Language	T/Th	7:00–9:00
Spanish I	M/W	7:00–9:00
Spanish II	T/Th	6:30–8:30
Spanish III	T/Th	8:30–10:00
Study Skills		
Speed Reading	M/Th	7:00–9:00
How to Study and Take Notes	T	7:00–9:00
How to Take Exams	W	7:00–9:00
Social Studies		
Citizenship	T/Th	7:00–9:00
U.S. Government	M	7:00–9:00
The U.S. Constitution	T	7:00–9:00
U.S. History	W	7:00–9:00
World History	Th	7:00–9:00
Business		
Typing I	T	6:30–9:30
Typing II	W	6:30–9:30
Bookkeeping	Th	6:30–9:30
Shorthand	M	6:30–9:30
Computer Programming	W	7:00–10:00
Word Processing I	M	6:30–9:30
Word Processing II	T	6:30–9:30
Business Math	Th	7:00–9:00
Business Writing	T	7:00–9:30
Skill Training for Employment		
Auto Mechanics	M	6:30–9:30
Machine Shop	W	6:30–9:30
Printing	Th	6:30–9:30
Radio & TV Repairs	W	6:30–9:30
Building Repairs	T	6:30–9:30
Food Service	Th	6:30–9:30
Blueprint Reading	T	6:30–9:30
Nurse's Aide/Orderly	M/Th	7:00–9:30

COURSE TITLE	Days*	Time
Art and Music		
Oil Painting	Th	7:00–9:30
Water Colors	W	7:30–10:00
Wood Carving	T	7:00–9:30
Picture Framing	M	7:00–9:30
Rug Hooking	W	7:00–9:30
Country Music U.S.A.	M	7:00–9:00
Music of Africa	Th	7:00–9:00
Home Care		
Sewing I	M	7:00–9:30
Sewing II	T	7:00–9:30
Sewing III	W	7:00–9:30
Home Improvements	Th	6:30–8:30
Cooking to Save Money	W	7:30–10:00
Cooking Around the World	Th	7:30–10:00
Gardening	M	7:00–9:00
Care of House Plants	T	7:00–9:00
Fire Safety in the Home	Th	7:00–9:00
Self Improvement		
Laws Everyone Should Know	T	7:00–9:00
Planning for Your Retirement	W	7:00–9:00
Parenting Skills	M	7:00–9:00
Great Books Discussion Group	Th	7:00–9:00
Driver Education	W	7:00–10:00
First Aid for Everyone	Th	7:30–9:30
Living with a Budget	M	7:00–9:00
Recreation		
Basketball for Fun, Men	T	7:00–10:00
Basketball for Fun, Women	Th	7:00–10:00
Bridge Playing	W	7:00–9:30
Square Dancing I	M	7:00–8:00
Square Dancing II	M	8:00–9:00
Dances of South America	W	7:00–8:30
Ballroom Dancing I	Th	7:00–8:00
Ballroom Dancing II	Th	8:00–9:00
Body Building	M/W	7:00–9:00
Swimming	T/Th	7:00–9:30
Boating Skills & Safety	W	7:30–9:30
Fresh Water Fishing	M	7:30–9:30

*Class Meeting Days: (M) Monday, (T) Tuesday, (W) Wednesday, (Th) Thursday

admit, educate (ej′ u cate), paragraph (pār′ u graph)

Fill in each blank with the correct form of the word given on the left.

educate	1. Mrs. Page wants to ____________________ her children.
education	Their ____________________ is very important to her.
admit	2. City College will not ____________________ any more students this fall.
admission	Sue will have to wait until next spring for ____________________.
decide	3. I have a hard ____________________ to make.
decision	I need to know more facts before I can ____________________.
register	4. Mrs. Dawson wants to fill out a ____________________ form
registration	so that she can ____________________ to vote.
pronounce	5. Joseph finds it hard to ____________________ some English words,
pronunciation	but his ____________________ is getting better.
apply	6. To ____________________ for a job at that factory,
application	you have to fill out an ____________________.
discuss	7. Last week, our ____________________ was about World War I.
discussion	Tonight, we will ____________________ World War II.
depress	8. Funny movies help me overcome ____________________.
depression	Sad movies ____________________ me even more.

Write a paragraph about one of these subjects.
Write the paragraph in your notebook.

1. What does education mean to you?
2. What do you do for recreation?
3. What was the hardest decision you ever made?

How to Use a Dictionary

noun	action	describe (dē scribe')	alphabet (al' phu bet)
verb	correct	guide (gide)	alphabetical (al phu bet' i cul)
adverb	entry	shown (shōn)	definition (def i ni' tion)
wee	sample	weight (wāt)	dictionary (dic' tion ār y)
weed		respell (rē spell')	adjective (ad' jec tiv)

How a Dictionary Can Help You

A dictionary is a book that tells you

- how words are spelled,
- how words are pronounced,
- how words are used, and
- the meanings of words.

How to Find Words

Alphabetical listing. In a dictionary, words are listed in order so that you can find them easily. Words are listed in the order of the letters of the alphabet. (The alphabet is shown at the bottom of this page.)

All words beginning with the letter *a* are listed in the first group of words. All words beginning with the letter *b* are listed in the second group of words, and so on, through the letter *z*.

Words beginning with the letters *a* through *e* are in the first third of the dictionary. Words beginning with *f* through *p* are in the middle third. And words beginning with *q* through *z* are in the last third of the dictionary.

All words having the same first letter are listed in order of their second letter, such as *club* and *coach*. All words with the same first and second letters are listed in order of their third letter, such as *coach* and *coin*.

Here is an example of some words listed in alphabetical order: *a, able, about, act, add, Africa, baby, back, bad, bag, band, bank, baseball*.

On the sample dictionary page shown here, you can see that the words in dark type are in alphabetical order.

Guide words. Two guide words are placed at the top of each page of a dictionary. The guide word at the top left shows you the first word listed on that page. The guide word at the top right shows you the last word listed on that page.

Aa Bb Cc Dd Ee Ff Gg Hh Ii Jj Kk Ll Mm Nn Oo Pp Qq Rr Ss Tt Uu Vv Ww Xx Yy Zz

Sample Page of a Dictionary

way ***noun*** (wā) 1. a road or path that leads from one place to another. *Which is the fastest way home?* 2. an opening that lets you move in or out of something. *The front door is the only way into the house.* 3. a particular direction. *Look that way to see the parade.* 4. a distance. *The store is just a short way from here.* 5. a manner; way of acting. *He spoke in a friendly way.* 6. a means of doing something; how to do something. *Do you know a good way to cook fish? | We need a way to solve this problem.*
by the way used to add something into a conversation that is on a different subject. *By the way, did you know there is no school on Friday?*

we ***pron.*** (wē) the person speaking or writing and one or more others. *We are friends.*

weak ***adj.*** (wēk) having little strength or power. *I felt weak after being sick. | We could hardly hear his weak voice.*

> **Word Builder: weak +**
> **weakness** (1): the state of being weak.
> **weakness** (2): a special liking for something.

wealth ***noun*** (welth) [N] a large amount of money or property. *She has money because of the wealth of her grandparents.*

> **Word Builder: wealth +**
> **wealthy:** having a lot of wealth; rich.

weapon ***noun*** (we pən) an object used to attack or defend. *Guns and bombs are weapons of war.*

wear ***verb*** (wār) ***wore, worn*** 1. to have or carry on your body. *He likes to wear rings. | She is wearing a skirt.* 2. to become damaged through long use. *The roof is beginning to wear.*
wear off to become less or disappear over time. *The ink marks will wear off in a few days.*
wear out to make or become useless through a lot of use. *He wore out his shoes.*

weather ***noun*** (we thər) [N] conditions outside. Weather includes temperature, rain, snow, sun, and other things. *What is the weather like in Chicago today? | I don't like this hot weather!*

weave ***verb*** (wēv) ***wove, woven*** to make cloth by passing threads over and under each other. *This machine weaves cotton for jeans. | She is weaving a rug.*

web ***noun*** (web) 1. a thin, open structure made of threads that connect to each other at points. *Many spiders make webs.* 2. [N] a short form of ***World Wide Web.***

wedding ***noun*** (we ding) a ceremony of marriage. *My sister's wedding will take place in a church.*

Wednesday ***noun*** (wenz dā) the fourth day of the week. Wednesday comes between Tuesday and Thursday.

weed ***noun*** (wēd) any plant that grows wild in places where people do not want it to grow. *We pulled weeds from our garden. | Weeds are a problem for farmers.*
verb to clear of weeds. *We weed our vegetable garden every week.*

week ***noun*** (wēk) a standard unit used to measure time. One week equals seven days.

weekday ***noun*** (wēk dā) any day of the week except Saturday and Sunday. *We go to school on weekdays.*

weekend ***noun*** (wēk end) the part of the week between Friday evening and Sunday evening. *We went to my grandmother's house over the weekend.*

weekly ***adj.*** (wēk lē) happening or appearing once a week. *We made our weekly trip to the supermarket. | She reads a weekly magazine.*
adv. once a week; each week. *She takes piano lessons weekly.*

weevil ***noun*** (wē vəl) a kind of insect that eats plants. The weevil is a problem for farmers who grow cotton.

weigh ***verb*** (wā) 1. to measure how heavy a person or thing is by using a scale. *The clerk weighed the cheese.* 2. to have a particular amount of weight. *I weigh ten pounds more than I did last year.*

weigh

weight ***noun*** (wāt) 1. [N] the quality that makes something heavy. *There is too much weight in the back of the boat.* 2. how heavy something is. *What is your weight? You look thin.*

welcome ***interj.*** (wel kəm) used to express warm greetings to someone who has just arrived. *Welcome! We're glad you could come.*
noun a warm greeting. *We gave her a warm welcome.*
verb to express pleasure and kind feelings when someone arrives or joins you. *We welcomed the new people to our office.*
adj. allowed to do something if you want. *You are welcome to share this food.*

Guide words help you find the word you want quickly and easily. For example, on the sample page, the first word is *way,* and the last word is *welcome*. If you're looking for *wet,* you know right away that it comes after this page.

Entry words. The words that are listed in the dictionary in alphabetical order are called entry words. Entry words stand out on the page because they are printed in dark type. The information about each entry word is printed in lighter type.

Example of how to find a word. How do you find the word *weigh* in a dictionary? You know that the first letter, *w,* is near the end of the alphabet. Open your dictionary to the last third of the pages. Turn to pages showing words that begin with *w*. Then look for pages with guide words beginning with *we*. Then choose a page with guide words that *weigh* would come between. On the sample dictionary page, *weigh* comes between the guide words *way* and *welcome*. Look down the page to find the entry word *weigh*.

How to Spell Words

Letters for sounds. To check a word for the correct spelling, pronounce the word slowly, and listen to its sounds. Think what letters stand for the sounds of the word. Then look for an entry word having those letters. Entry words are spelled correctly.

Some words sound alike, but they are spelled differently for different meanings. For example, the word *way* and the word *weigh* sound the same but have different meanings. Look for the word you want according to the way you think it is spelled. Read the meaning shown for the word. If it is not the word you want, then think of another way the word might be spelled.

Word endings. You may want to check the correct spelling of a word in a different form. You may not find the word listed as an entry word. But you can find it on the line next to the entry word in root form. For example, after the entry word *weave* are shown *wove* and *woven*.

How to Pronounce Words

Syllables and stress. Entry words are shown with dots between syllables. Then, each entry word is respelled to show how it sounds and which syllables are stressed.

Pronunciation key. At the front of most dictionaries is a pronunciation key. It tells you how each consonant and vowel sound will be shown in the respellings of entry words. The pronunciation key gives a list of short, easy words as examples of the sounds.

How to Find Word Meanings

Parts of speech. A dictionary shows the way a word is used by giving its part of speech. The parts of speech used most often are:

n. — noun (name of person, place, or thing)
n. pl. — noun plural
v. — verb (action word)
adj. — adjective (word that describes a noun, or name word)
adv. — adverb (word that describes a verb, or action word)

As an example, the word *weed* as a noun has a different meaning from the word *weed* as a verb.

Definitions. A definition of a word gives the meaning of the word. A dictionary gives one or more definitions for each entry word.

As an example, for the word *way,* the sample page of the dictionary shows six definitions for *way* as a noun.

Sometimes you will need to read all of the definitions for a word to find the meaning of the word for the sentence you are reading.

Examples of how words are used. The dictionary helps you understand some definitions by giving examples of how the words are used. See the following:

week, noun — One week equals seven days.

welcome, adj. — You are welcome to share this food.

Story Checkup

Study the sample dictionary page, and answer these questions.

1. What two words does *Wednesday* come between? ______________________________

2. What compound words beginning with *week* are listed as entry words?

   ______________________________ ______________________________

3. What word with an ending is shown for *welcome* as a verb? ______________________

4. What is a *weevil*? ________________ What part of speech is it? ______________

5. How many meanings are there for the word *weigh* as a verb? ____________________

   Write a sentence using the word *weigh* as a verb. ______________________________

   ____

6. What entry word has the ending *-ing*? ______________________________

   What part of speech is it? ______________________________

7. Write the words that are made by adding the endings *-er* and *-est* to *weak*.

   ______________________________ ______________________________

8. Write the way to pronounce the word *weave*. ______________________________

9. Is the word *wash* listed on the sample dictionary page? ______________________

   Why or why not? ______________________________

These words sound alike, but they are spelled differently, and they have different meanings. Read the words. Then write the correct word in each blank.

(weed, we'd) 1. ____________________ like to know if this plant is a flower or a ____________________.

(hall, haul) 2. The men took the boxes from the front ____________________ of our house. They loaded the boxes into their truck to ____________________ them away.

(wait, weight) 3. I'll ____________________ until I've lost ____________________ before I buy a new coat.

(way, weigh) 4. A truck driver must ____________________ his truck and its load on the ____________________ to market.

(peace, piece) 5. Ann ate a ____________________ of chocolate cake in the ____________________ and quiet of the empty kitchen.

(threw, through) 6. Ed ____________________ the ball ____________________ the basket and got the first two points of the basketball game.

(flower, flour) 7. Joyce bought eggs, butter, milk, and ____________________ to make a birthday cake. Then she bought some roses at a ____________________ shop.

(chews, choose) 8. Which pet would you ____________________ to have, a cat that claws your sofa and chairs or a puppy that ____________________ on everything?

Add *re-* to the beginning of each root word. Write the new word in the blank.

Example: spell respell

1. read ____________________
2. write ____________________
3. turn ____________________
4. pay ____________________
5. open ____________________
6. marry ____________________

Fill in each blank with one of the new words with *re-*.

1. I have to ____________________ that loan in six months.
2. My mother never wanted to ____________________ after my father died.
3. I'll let you use my car if you ____________________ it by six o'clock.

Write the words in each list in the correct alphabetical order.

List 1		List 2	
alphabet	____________	describe	____________
adjective	____________	dumb	____________
action	____________	definition	____________
adverb	____________	does	____________
adult	____________	dictionary	____________

Read the guide words at the top of each list of words given below. In each list, underline the words that would be found on the same page as the two guide words.

face — father	safe — speed	grade — guide
fact	same	guest
fair	sauce	gym
fence	salute	grew
fame	sample	good
false	save	graduate
fault	said	gun

Copy the entry words that have more than one syllable from the sample dictionary page. Don't copy a word with an ending unless it is listed as an entry word.

____________ ____________ ____________

____________ ____________ ____________

____________ ____________ ____________

Which syllable has the main stress in all of these words? ____________

Study Helps for *People and Places*

George Washington Carver

done (dun)	gone (gawn)	steal

Discuss the answers to these questions.

1. What handicaps did George Carver have as a child?
2. What helped him overcome these handicaps?
3. Why did George Carver accept the job offer from Tuskegee Institute?
4. What problems did George Carver find at Tuskegee Institute?
5. What did Professor Carver do to overcome these problems?
6. Why did Professor Carver think it was important to find new uses for peanuts, sweet potatoes, and pecans?
7. Why did Congress make a national monument of George Carver's birthplace?

Write a short answer to each question.

1. What skills did George Carver learn as a boy that helped him get through school?

 ____

2. In what three states did George Carver go to school?

 ____

3. Where is Tuskegee Institute? ______________________________
4. Who did George Carver turn to when he had a problem? ______________________________

Circle the right form of the verb to complete the sentence.

Example: I have not (do, did, (done)) my homework yet.

1. Night riders (steal, stole, stolen) George Carver's mother.
2. The Carvers were the only parents that George ever (know, knew, known).
3. George felt that his work was never (do, did, done).
4. The farmers were (show, showed, shown) how to improve their soil.
5. Professor Carver (takes, took, taken) peanuts into his lab and locked the door.
6. The farmers will (grow, grew, grown) a different crop next year.
7. Have you ever (go, went, gone) to the Carver Museum at Tuskegee?

Terry Fox

Discuss the answers to these questions.

1. What made Terry Fox feel sorry for himself?
2. What happened to help him change his outlook on life?
3. Why do you think Terry's marathon brought in money for cancer research?
4. Why didn't Terry take the shortest way across Canada?
5. Why did Terry stop his run?
6. Do you think Terry's run across Canada was a good idea? Why or why not?

Write a short answer to each question.

1. What was Terry Fox's run across Canada called? ______________________________
2. From what ocean did he start his run? ______________________________

   What ocean did he hope to reach? ______________________________
3. How many miles did Terry try to run each day? ______________________________
4. For about how many months did Terry run? ______________________________
5. How many miles across Canada did Terry run? ______________________________
6. In what province did Terry's run end? ______________________________
7. How much money did the Marathon of Hope raise for cancer research? ______________

Write the missing ending in each blank.

-ful -less -ly -ment -ness

1. When he first learned that he had cancer, Terry felt hope__________.
2. Terry needed cancer treat__________.
3. Until he learned to walk with his artificial leg, Terry felt help__________.
4. During his training, Terry ran exact__________ 3,419 miles.
5. Terry's running was pain__________ to watch.
6. Terry had to stop his marathon because of pain and weak__________.
7. After cancer struck a second time, Terry tried to keep a cheer__________ outlook.
8. Terry said, "Maybe the sick__________ beat my body, but it couldn't touch my spirit."

Study Helps for *People and Places*

Sacajawea

Discuss the answers to these questions.

1. Describe Sacajawea when Lewis and Clark met her.
2. What was the reason for the Lewis and Clark Expedition?
3. Why did Lewis and Clark want Sacajawea to go with them?
4. What did Sacajawea do for the expedition?
5. What was the hardest part of the journey and why?
6. Why was the Lewis and Clark Expedition important in U.S. history?
7. How did Captain Clark thank Sacajawea for her help?

Write a short answer to each question.

1. What did Sacajawea's name mean? ______________________________
2. What mountains did the Indians call the Shining Mountains? ______________________________
3. When did the United States buy the Louisiana Territory? ______________________________
4. Who was the U.S. president at that time? ______________________________
5. When did the Lewis and Clark Expedition leave St. Louis? ______________________________
6. How did Sacajawea carry her baby on the journey? ______________________________
7. What land did the explorers claim for the United States? ______________________________

In each line, circle the word that does not belong with the other three.

Example:	trader	explorer	(summer)	leader
1.	horse	buffalo	boll weevil	elephant
2.	city	town	village	nation
3.	guide	chief	captain	fort
4.	Clark	Spanish	English	French
5.	storm	ocean	waterfall	river
6.	pecans	blankets	peanuts	berries
7.	walk	steep	dance	run
8.	Oregon	Missouri	Sacajawea	Louisiana

Frank C. Laubach

Discuss the answers to these questions.

1. Why was Dr. Laubach's literacy program in Lanao in danger?
2. How did the Maranao people keep their literacy program going?
3. How did the literacy program help the Maranao people?
4. Why was Dr. Laubach called the "Apostle to the Illiterates"?
5. How did Frank Laubach find inner peace and strength?
6. What problems of illiterates of the world did Dr. Laubach describe in his speeches?
7. What did Frank C. Laubach do to help the illiterates of the world?

Write a short answer to each question.

1. In what country did Each One Teach One begin? ______________________________
2. In what year did Each One Teach One begin? ______________________________
3. Whose idea was it? ______________________________
4. Who did Dr. Laubach call the "Silent Billion"? ______________________________
5. Give the title of a book by Frank Laubach. ______________________________
6. What group named for him carries on his work in the country where you live?

   ____

Match each word in the first list with a word in the second list that means the opposite. Write the letter in the blank. The first one is done for you.

D	1. soft	A. toward
_____	2. birth	B. remember
_____	3. tiny	C. peace
_____	4. war	D. hard
_____	5. forget	E. minor
_____	6. weak	F. huge
_____	7. literate	G. death
_____	8. friendly	H. smooth
_____	9. apart	I. illiterate
_____	10. away from	J. powerful
_____	11. rough	K. together
_____	12. major	L. unfriendly

This book introduces the 707 words and 7 symbols listed below. Variants formed by adding *-s, -es, -'s, -s', -ed, -ing, -er, -est, -y,* and *-ly* to previously taught words are not listed, even when *y* is changed to *i* before an ending. New words are listed in their root form when they are used with these previously taught endings. Italics indicate that a word taught earlier is reintroduced in this book as a key word for a particular sound and spelling. A hyphenated word made from two previously taught words is not listed as new.

The correlated readers, *People and Places* and *More Stories 4,* introduce additional words. Those words are listed in the back of the books. Lessons to accompany *People and Places* use some of those words, but they are not listed in this book.

Word	Lesson
about	9
above	5
accept	18
accident	12
according	16
ache	19
across	12
action	21
addition	20
adjective	21
admission	20
admit	20
adult	19
adverb	21
advertise	16
afraid	1
Africa	19
African	19
afternoon	3
against	10
aid	18
aide	16
airplane	1
alike	10
all	13
allow	11
almost	15
along	12
alphabet	21
alphabetical	21
also	13
although	19
always	15
American	14
amuse	1
amusement	20
animal	7
annoy	15
apply	15
appointment	19
aren't	2
argue	2
army	18
around	9
art	20
Asia	19
Asian	19
aspirin	17
Aug.	16
August	13
aunt	2
auto	12
automobile	12
Ave.	9
avenue	6
avoid	15
awful	12
ball	13
ballroom	20
bandage	18
barbecue	2
bark	12
baseball	13
basketball	13
beat	17
beaten	17
beautiful	8
because	12
become	1
bedroom	3
begin	3
believe	6
belong	16
between	14
birthday	6
bite	19
blank	1
blood	19
blue	4
blueprint	20
board	7
body	19
book	8
bookkeeping	20
bottom	16
bought	14
boy	15
Branch	13
breathe	2
bridge	18
brook	8
Brooklyn	13
brought	14
Brown	10
Brunoski	11
budget	20
bugle	4
bull	19
Bush	8
business	1
cabin	8
calendar	6
California	13
call	13
cancer	7
carve	8
case	19
catch	8
caught	14
cause	12
central	17
chance	13
Chang	18
chapter	8
Charles	17
Charlotte	17
chef	17
chemistry	17
chest	19
Chevy	17
chew	5
Chicago	17
chip	17
chocolate	17
choke	2
choose	17
chorus	17
chose	17
Chris	17
Christmas	13
citizenship	18
classified	16
classroom	14
claw	12
climb	7
clinic	19
clown	10
club	4
coach	6
coin	15
company	7
complete	12
compound	13
computer	1
concert	4
consonant	17
constitution	20
contents	8
contest	10
continue	2
contraction	6
cook	8
cookie	17
cool	5
correct	21
cough	19
could	8
couldn't	12
council	9
county	10
course	20
courthouse	9
cousin	2
cow	10
crack	13
crawl	12
crew	5
crowd	10
crumb	19
cuffs	17
cure	1
daily	7
damage	12
dance	20
D'Angelo	20
danger	18
daughter	14
Dawson	12
daytime	4
Dec.	20
December	13
decide	20
decision	20
deep	19
definition	21
Democratic	18
deposit	3
depress	16
depression	20
describe	21

Word	Lesson
desk	14
destroy	15
dictionary	21
difference	18
different	16
dig	12
diploma	20
direct	19
direction	19
dirt	5
disappoint	15
discuss	9
discussion	20
Dodgers	13
doesn't	17
dog	12
done	22
dose	19
down	10
downtown	15
drove	10
drum	4
Duke	6
dumb	19
during	15
east	9
easy	10
edge	18
editor	16
editorial	16
educate	20
education	20
election	18
electric	11
elephant	19
emergency	5
employ	15
employee	15
employment	15
enemy	18
energy	18
enjoy	15
enroll	18
entry	21
everywhere	1
exam	19
example	1
excite	10
excuse (v.)	17
exit	12
experience	15
fact	1
fair	10
fall	13
false	13
fame	13
fan	13
fault	12
February	13
feet	10
female	16
fence	12
few	2
fifth	9
fireworks	4
fist	2
flag	4
flour	17
flower	10
flute	4
fog	12
food	3
foot	8
football	13
Ford	12
forever	3
form	1
fought	14
found	9
Fri.	16
front	12
frown	10
full	8
furnished	3
game	1
gas	17
Gene	18
gentle	18
Ginger	18
given	7
Gladys	11
goes	4
gone	22
good	8
Gordon	18
government	20
Grace	18
grade	15
graduate	18
grand	16
grandchildren	14
grandfather	2
grandmother	2
grew	5
ground	9
group	7
grow	5
grown	19
guest	20
guide	21
gym	17
hall	13
haul	12
haven't	2
headache	19
headline	7
health	16
heart	4
heat	3
held	10
hello	20
here's	17
highway	12
history	20
hole	12
holiday	4
homeroom	17
honor	4
hook	8
Hoover	3
hopeless	15
horse	10
horseback	11
hour	16
house	9
housing	9
how	10
Howard	10
hug	2
huge	1
Hugh	2
human	1
Huron	2
I	20
II	20
III	20
I'd	17
important	19
improvement	20
information	5
insect	19
insurance	12
interest	6
isn't	3
issue	17
Italy	20
I've	15
ivory	19
Jackie	13
Jake	8
January	6
Jerry	12
jewels	5
Johnson	15
Johnstown	10
join	15
Joseph	20
Joyce	15
Judy	5
July	4
June	4
Kansas	17
kept	13
knee	19
kneel	19
knew	6
knob	19
knock	19
lab	19
laid	15
land	11
landlord	3
language	4
laundry	12
law	12
lawn	12
lay	18
leaf	4
league	13
leaves	5
leftover	5
less	15
Lewis	5
limb	19
lion	7
loan	9
loaves	11
long	12
lost	16
low	9
Luke	5
lunchroom	17
machine	1
mail	18
main	4
major	13
male	16
manager	13
maple	4
math	6
mean	1
measure	17
mechanic	17
medic	18
medicine	19
meet	4
mental	16
mess	16
Michael	17
middle	18
might	15
million	10
mind	3
minor	19
minute	2
Mitchell	17
mix	17
Mon.	16
moon	17
mountain	9
mouth	9
move	3
movie	16
music	1
nation	20
national	13
neighbor	9
neighborhood	9
nephew	2
Newman	6
news	6
newspaper	6
niece	2
no.	12
noise	15
non-prescription	19
noon	3
note	8
notebook	8
notice	17
noun	21
November	13
now	10
nut	17
object (n.)	2
occasion	18
occupation	18
off	12
offer	16
often	14

Word	Lesson
Ohio	12
oil	15
once	19
¼ (one fourth)	17
½ (one half)	17
only	8
opposite	5
O'Toole	3
ought	14
our	9
out	9
overdose	19
page	7
pain	19
parade	4
paragraph	20
passenger	17
Paul	12
peaceful	19
pencil	14
per	4
physical	19
physician	19
pickup	5
picnic	4
pie	10
piece	2
plant	8
pleasant	17
pleasure	17
plow	11
plural	11
point	15
political	18
pool	3
poor	5
pound	19
power	11
prejudice	13
prescription	19
present	18
president	7
press	2
pressure	17
print	1
problem	9
process	20
program	17
pronounce	20
pronunciation	20
proud	9
public	5
pull	8
push	8
quiet	3
rate	7
reach	19
rear	12
reason	20
recipe	17
record (n.)	1
recreation	20
redness	19
refuse (v.)	2
register	18
registration	18
relative	2
remark	17
remove	4
report	5
Republican	18
rescue	2
residence	18
respell	21
retirement	20
reunion	2
rib	2
ribbon	10
rich	5
Rickey	13
Robinson	13
rode	17
room	3
roommate	3
root	3
rope	7
rough	19
Roy	15
rude	4
rule	4
safe	3
safety	20
salt	17
salute	4
sample	21
sauce	12
saw	12
schedule	17
school	3
scream	18
season	13
section	16
security	1
seem	17
seen	2
self	16
Sept.	16
September	13
series	13
sew	20
sewer	5
sharp	16
Shaw	12
shine	17
shook	15
shoot	18
shortening	17
shorthand	20
should	11
shout	9
shown	21
sidewalk	16
sift	17
signature	15
silent	19
since	2
sixth	9
skill	20
skin	19
slept	15
small	13
smooth	19
soap	19
social	1
soda	17
soft	17
soldier	18
soon	3
sorry	12
south	9
space	1
spaceship	1
Spanish	20
speech	17
spell	19
spoon	17
spray	19
spring	13
square	20
St.	9
star	4
station	20
steal	22
step	5
stir	17
stove	8
strange	18
stress	1
stripe	4
strong	12
student	6
stupid	6
subject	20
such	17
Sue	10
sugar	8
summer	10
Sunday	3
support	15
sure	10
swim	3
tablet	19
taken	19
tale	18
talk	13
taught	14
teaspoon	17
television	20
thankful	16
Thanksgiving	13
themselves	18
they'll	15
they're	20
thick	19
those	3
thought	14
thousand	9
¾ (three fourths)	17
threw	5
through	16
thumb	19
Thursday	4
ticket	14
title	8
together	3
tomato	12
too	3
took	8
tooth	11
tough	19
town	10
toy	15
track	13
tractor	10
Tran Ty Lan	14
transportation	20
trash	5
trouble	14
true	4
trunk	19
truth	15
Tuesday	6
tusk	19
tutor	6
⅔ (two thirds)	17
type	20
understood	8
unemployed	15
unemployment	15
unfurnished	3
unhappy	10
unless	19
unpleasant	17
until	5
unusual	19
use (v.)	1
usual	17
usually	17
utilities	3
vanilla	17
verb	21
Vietnam	14
view	2
voice	15
vowel	11
walk	14
wall	13
war	14
warn	19
wash	16
watchdog	12
wave	2
we'd	20
Wednesday	6
weed	21
weigh	19
weight	21
welcome	17
west	9
wet	12
win	10
winter	7
wish	7
without	9
Wong	14
woods	8
worry	15
would	8
wouldn't	17
wound (woond)	18
wrap	19
wrinkle	19
wrong	15
zoo	4